D0458931

THE
MEASURE
OF OUR
HEARTS

THE
MEASURE
OF OUR
HEARTS

MARVIN J. ASHTON

Deseret Book Company
Salt Lake City, Utah

Acknowledgements

Special thanks to the following associates at Deseret Book who helped in the preparation and publication of this book: Ronald A. Millett, president and general manager; Eleanor Knowles, vice president and executive editor; Sheri L. Dew, director of publishing; and Kent Ware, design director. I also appreciate the assistance of my very competent secretary, Randi Greene.

© 1991 Marvin J. Ashton

All rights reserved. No part of this book may be reproduced in any form or by any means without permission in writing from the publisher, Deseret Book Company, P.O. Box 30178, Salt Lake City, Utah 84130. This work is not an official publication of The Church of Jesus Christ of Latter-day Saints. The views expressed herein are the responsibility of the author and do not necessarily represent the position of the Church or of Deseret Book Company.

Deseret Book is a registered trademark of Deseret Book Company.

Library of Congress Cataloging-in-Publication Data

Ashton, Marvin J., 1915–
    The measure of our hearts / Marvin J. Ashton.
      p. cm.
    Includes index.
    ISBN 0-87579-564-1
    1. Spiritual life—Mormon authors. 2. Church of Jesus Christ of Latter-day Saints—Doctrines. 3. Mormon Church—Doctrines.
I. Title.
BX8656.A827   1991
248.4'89332—dc20   91–24969
                                                       CIP

Printed in the United States of America

10   9   8   7   6   5   4   3   2   1

Contents

CHAPTER 1

The Measure of Our Hearts

A measurement is a standard by which we determine the capacity or dimension of a person or object. A measurement gives us a basis for comparison.

If I say, "She is a three-point student," you will have a pretty good idea of this person's scholastic ability. A measurement may also be an estimate of what is expected of an individual.

Human measurement, of course, is subject to human fallibility. My generation, for example, was taught that a person's I.Q. was supposedly a fixed measurement of a person's capacity to learn. Such a notion is now generally discredited by the teaching profession. Interestingly, the Prophet Joseph Smith taught in the nineteenth century: "We consider that God has created man with a mind capable of instruction, and a faculty which may be enlarged in proportion to the heed and diligence given to the light communicated from heaven to the intellect." (*Teachings of the Prophet Joseph Smith*, p. 51.) He was obviously ahead of his time!

We also tend to evaluate others on the basis of physical, outward appearance: their appearance, their social status, their family pedigrees, their degrees, or their economic situations.

The Lord, however, has a different standard by which he measures a person. When it came time to choose a king to replace King Saul, the Lord gave this criterion to his prophet Samuel: "Look not on his countenance, or on the height of his stature; . . . for the Lord seeth not as man seeth; for man looketh on the outward appearance, but the Lord looketh on the heart." (1 Samuel 16:7.)

When the Lord measures an individual, he does not use a tape measure around the person's head to determine his mental capacity, nor around his chest to determine his manliness. He measures the heart as an indicator of the person's capacity and potential to bless others.

Why the heart? Because the heart is a symbol of one's entire makeup. We often use phrases about the heart to describe the total person. Thus, we describe people as being "big-hearted" or "goodhearted" or having "a heart of gold." Or we speak of people with faint hearts, wise hearts, pure hearts, willing hearts, deceitful hearts, conniving hearts, courageous hearts, cold hearts, hearts of stone, or selfish hearts.

The measure of our hearts is the measure of our total performance. As the term is used by the Lord, our hearts describe our efforts to better ourselves or others or the conditions we confront.

A question I suggest is this: How do we measure up? Ultimately we will be judged not only for our actions, but also for the desires of our hearts. This truth was revealed to the Prophet Joseph Smith at a time when he was shown in vision the celestial kingdom. The revelation is recorded

2

in section 137 of the Doctrine and Covenants. Joseph marveled when he saw his deceased brother Alvin in the celestial kingdom, for Alvin had died before the gospel was restored. Joseph then received this great truth: "All who have died without a knowledge of this gospel, who would have received it if they had been permitted to tarry, shall be heirs of the celestial kingdom of God; . . . for I, the Lord, will judge all men according to their works, according to the desire of their hearts." (D&C 137:7, 9.)

If our works and the desires of our hearts are the ultimate criteria of our character, how do we measure up? What kind of heart should we seek? For what kind of heart should we pray? How should we measure the worth of other people?

May I suggest four questions that deal with the heart that may help us determine how we are measuring up.

1. *How honest in heart am I?*

We pray that our missionaries will find the honest in heart. What does it mean to be honest in heart? It means to be open to truth and to evaluate information or people without prejudice. Honest-hearted persons are individuals without pretense, without hypocrisy. They are reliable in word and action. They have no hidden agendas to deceive others or to misrepresent facts. In contrast, those with conniving hearts will deceive and misrepresent.

An honest heart will lead to a change of heart. Spiritually speaking, a change of heart is not only desirable but also essential for eternal life. The Book of Mormon describes the conversion experience, which all of us must have, as a "mighty change in us, or in our hearts, that we have no more disposition to do evil, but to do good continually." (Mosiah 5:2.)

The Book of Mormon is a study of interesting contrasts between those who hardened their hearts and those whose hearts were softened by the Spirit of the Lord. How does one have his or her heart softened under the influence of the Holy Ghost? Nephi's testimony provides an answer: "Having great desires to know of the mysteries of God, wherefore, I did cry unto the Lord; and behold *he did . . . soften my heart* that I did believe all the words which had been spoken by my father." (1 Nephi 2:16; italics added.)

After obtaining a testimony of the gospel and the Lord's church, we should then strive to become pure in heart. This will result in happiness and eventually the promise of a society without contention. It is the Savior's way to peace.

2. *Do I have a willing heart?*

Let us look again to the scriptures for guidance: "Behold, the Lord requireth the heart and a willing mind; and the willing and obedient shall eat the good of the land of Zion in these last days." (D&C 64:34.)

A willing heart describes one who desires to please the Lord and to serve the Lord's cause first. He serves the Lord on the Lord's terms, not his own. There are no restrictions to where or how he will serve.

As one who has tendered calls to serve to many, I am always pleased to see members willing to give their time, energy, and effort to the upbuilding of the Church. They do so primarily for one reason: to serve the Lord with all their heart, might, mind, and strength.

I have a friend who served as a priests quorum adviser. The boys and the adviser planned a kayak activity at Flaming Gorge, Utah. After some initial planning, one of the quorum members quietly approached the adviser and said, "We'd better not plan a kayak trip. Mike won't be able to go because he can't paddle." Mike was partially paralyzed on his right side. When he learned that the quorum was not going on the activity because of him, he told the boys, "I want to go. I can paddle." The adviser placed his hand on Mike's shoulder and said, "OK, Mike. You're my paddle partner."

From January to August, the boys built their kayaks. They departed to the reservoir the first week in August.

Rhythm, togetherness, and teamwork are essential to keep a kayak in a straight line. Mike and his partner had more trouble than the others getting their rhythm and strokes coordinated. Mike had almost no stroke of consequence on his right side, so his adviser had to compensate by paddling easy on the left and hard on the right. After several hours of learning to work together, Mike said, "You wouldn't happen to have a Band-Aid, would you?" The adviser pulled his wallet out and gave him a Band-Aid. Mike placed it over a big water blister that had just popped in the crook of his hand between his thumb and his first finger. The hand and arm that were little used now had to help hold the paddle.

Several hours later, Mike turned again to his adviser, who was in the rear cockpit, and said, "Do you have any more bandages?" The adviser pulled out several and handed them to him. By now the crook between Mike's right thumb and his first finger was becoming raw. Mike applied the Band-Aids and resumed paddling.

The next day the crew set out again. The adviser encouraged Mike to rest from paddling and let his hand have a respite. The words fell on deaf ears. Instantly Mike was paddling as he had the day before.

This day, a midday and afternoon wind blew directly at the flotilla of kayak paddlers, which meant they had to use stronger strokes and expend greater energy and time. Wincing with pain, Mike continued to paddle. Each suggestion that he rest intensified his will to carry his load.

Throughout the week, Mike persisted in holding his own. Though his hand had become as raw as hamburger, he would not give up. During the week's trip, the conversation with his senior companion often centered around his desire to go on a mission. Repeatedly he asked, "I hope they'll let me go on a mission. Do you think my problem will prevent me from going?" Mike walks with a noticeable limp of his right leg. He has a firm handshake with the left hand, but his right hand doesn't open up all the way.

How many who have no visible blemish have a heart like Mike's? How many with not a single cell out of place fail to soften their hearts and desire to serve the Lord? How many who have so much forfeit their blessings because of selfish desires or inability to set lofty priorities?

My adviser friend said, "Mike taught eleven others that though one may appear to be a little less physically able, the heart makes the difference in those who choose to overcome many odds and set a standard for others to follow."

Mike fulfilled an honorable mission to California and is now working in his hometown. What does the Lord require for service? A willing heart and an intense desire.

3. *Do I have an understanding, loving heart?*

An understanding, loving heart is the pinnacle of all human emotions. As the Apostle Paul said, charity "beareth all things, believeth all things, hopeth all things, endureth all things." (1 Corinthians 13:7.) We come closest to becoming Christlike when we are charitable and understanding of others. We will never approach godliness until we learn to love and lift. Indifference to others and their plight denies us life's sweetest moments of joy and service.

4. *"If ye have experienced a change of heart, and if ye have felt to sing the song of redeeming love, . . . can ye feel so now?"* (Alma 5:26.)

Having a change of heart at one time in our lives is insufficient to give us an understanding heart today. Helping and understanding a person years ago do not fill us with the love of God today. Christlike love must be continuous and contemporary.

One night a young idealist had a dream. He dreamed there was a new store in a nearby shopping mall. He went in and saw an angel behind a counter. Nervously, he asked what the shop sold. "Everything your heart desires," replied the angel. "Then I want peace on earth," said the idealist. "I want an end to famine, sorrow, and disease." "Just a moment," replied the angel. "You haven't understood. We don't sell fruit here—only seeds."

I pray that God will give each of us the courage and desire to strive for a pure heart, a willing heart, an understanding and loving heart. May we take the seeds offered to us, plant them, and nourish them so that we may help harvest the matured fruit of the gospel of Jesus Christ.

If we can do this, our measurements will not be found deficient when the final judgment is made and our hearts are measured by the Lord. The gospel of Jesus Christ has the power to change hearts and help individuals become pure, gentle, honest, kind, and loving.

7

CHAPTER 2

"I Would Be Worthy"

In recent weeks I have had some conversations that have made me ponder the meaning of the word *worthy*. As I talked to a twenty-year-old man, I discussed his attitude about going on a mission. He said, "I wanted to go, but I'm not worthy." "Who made that judgment?" I asked. "I did," was his answer.

On another occasion I asked a young lady who was contemplating marriage if she was going to the temple. She said, "I'd like to, but I am not worthy." In response to the same question of who determined her unworthiness, she too said, "I did."

A mother who had known for many weeks that her daughter had planned a temple marriage was asked if she were going to attend the temple ceremony. "No. I'm not worthy to get a temple recommend," she answered.

Each of these people seemed to have made his or her own determination about worthiness. We do not have to be hindered by self-judgment. All of us have the benefit and added wisdom of a bishop and a stake president to help us determine our worthiness and, if necessary, to assist us in beginning the process of becoming worthy to accomplish whatever goal we wish to achieve. When we take it upon ourselves to pass self-judgment and simply declare, "I'm not worthy," we build a barrier to progress and erect blockades that prevent our moving forward. We are not being fair when we judge ourselves. A second and third opinion will always be helpful and proper.

It occurs to me that many do not understand what worthiness is. Worthiness is a process, while perfection is an eternal trek. We can be worthy to enjoy certain privileges without being perfect.

Perhaps it is reasonable to conclude that personal measurement or judgment oftentimes may be severe and inaccurate. We may get bogged down when we try to understand and define *worthiness*. All of us are particularly aware of our shortcomings and weaknesses. Therefore, it is easy for us to feel that we are unworthy of blessings we desire and that we are not as worthy to hold an office or calling as someone else may be.

Throughout life we meet people who tell of their weaknesses with great enthusiasm and unreasonable prejudice. They may not report untruths, but they may leave out truths or they may not be fair with themselves. Misjudgments can be made. If we are to move forward wisely and think clearly, all sides of the story must be reviewed. When we feel inadequate, capable and loving friends can help us realize our strengths and potential.

When counseling, I have always tried to get the facts. Oftentimes those being interviewed resist sharing some of the facts because they make them uncomfortable. Worthy and lasting changes can be made only when actions are based upon the light of truth. People sometimes become comfortable in their self-declared unworthiness status.

Possibly the hardest guidelines for us to follow are those we set for ourselves. To analyze our fears, our dreams, our goals, and our motives can be soul-wrenching. We need others to help us. We may find that we fear failure so much that we won't take a risk. Our self-esteem may be bruised by criticism. Many other facts about ourselves may be brought to light in the process.

Perhaps we live under some misconceptions when we look at each other on Sundays at our meetings. We are all neatly dressed and greet each other with smiles. It is natural to assume that everyone else has life under control and doesn't have to deal with dark little weaknesses and imperfections.

There is a natural, probably a mortal, tendency for us to compare ourselves with others. Unfortunately, when we make comparisons, we tend to compare our weakest attributes with someone else's strongest. For example, a woman who feels unschooled in the gospel may be comparing herself with a woman who teaches the Gospel Doctrine class and seems to have every scripture at her fingertips. Obviously these kinds of comparisons are destructive and reinforce the fear that somehow we don't measure up and therefore we must not be as worthy as the next person.

We need to come to terms with our desire to reach perfection and our frustration when our accomplishments or behaviors are less than perfect. I believe that one of the great myths we would do well to dispel is that we have come to earth to perfect ourselves, and that nothing short of that will do. If I understand the teachings of the prophets of this dispensation correctly, we will not become perfect in this life, though we can make significant strides toward that goal.

10

Elder Joseph Fielding Smith offered this counsel: "Salvation does not come all at once; we are commanded to be perfect even as our Father in heaven is perfect. It will take us ages to accomplish this end, for there will be greater progress beyond the grave, and it will be there that the faithful will overcome all things, and receive all things, even the fulness of the Father's glory.

"I believe the Lord meant just what he said: that we should be perfect, as our Father in heaven is perfect. That will not come all at once, but line upon line, and precept upon precept, example upon example, and even then not as long as we live in this mortal life, for we will have to go even beyond the grave before we reach that perfection and shall be like God." (*Doctrines of Salvation,* 3 vols., Salt Lake City: Bookcraft, 1954–56, 2:18–19.)

I am also convinced that the speed with which we head along the straight and narrow path isn't as important as the direction in which we are traveling. That direction, if it is leading toward eternal goals, is the all-important factor.

Another quotation, which comes from President George Q. Cannon, is very meaningful to me: "Now, this is the truth. We humble people, we who feel ourselves sometimes so worthless, so good-for-nothing, we are not so worthless as we think. There is not one of us but what God's love has been expended upon. There is not one of us that He has not cared for and caressed. There is not one of us that He has not desired to save and that He has not devised means to save. There is not one of us that He has not given His angels charge concerning. We may be insignificant and contemptible in our own eyes and in the eyes of others, but the truth remains that we are children of God and that He has actually given His angels . . . charge concerning us, and they watch over us and have us in their keeping." (*Gospel Truths,* Classics in Mormon Literature Series, Salt Lake City: Deseret Book, 1987, pp. 3–4.)

If we are in the keeping of angels, God is certainly telling us that we are worthy to be watched over, helped, and directed by him. As we become aware of God's watch-care and as we turn to Church leaders to help us learn how to become worthy members of The Church of Jesus Christ of Latter-day Saints, we learn that we can reach the status of worthiness for each goal along life's path. Yet we must strive for worthiness.

In the Doctrine and Covenants is found Official Declaration–2, accepted by the Church on September 30, 1978. This revelation extends the priesthood to every *worthy* male member of the Church over age twelve. It reminds us that certain privileges have worthiness as a prerequisite. In this official declaration, the word *worthy* or *worthiness* is used six times. This leaves little doubt as to the importance of being worthy if specific blessings are to be available to us.

It is a wonderful strength and a needful process to be able to go to a bishop or a stake president and discuss our worthiness. During such interviews we may learn how worthiness can be achieved if there is need for improvement.

President N. Eldon Tanner gave us some wise counsel: "With all this evil present in the world today, it is most important that those who are responsible conduct proper interviews. Let us always remember that our main purpose, assignment, and responsibility is to save souls.

"It is important that those we interview realize that they are spirit children of God and that we love them, and let them know that we love them and are interested in their welfare and in helping them succeed in life.

"It is a great responsibility for a bishop or stake president to conduct a worthiness interview. There is equal responsibility, however, upon the member who is interviewed. Careful, searching interviews need to be conducted always individually and privately. . . . Let [the member] know that if there is something amiss in his life, there are ways to straighten it out. There is a great cleansing power of repentance. . . .

"You bishops and stake presidents might approach an interview for a temple recommend something like this: 'You have come to me for a recommend to enter the temple. I have the responsibility of representing the Lord in interviewing you. At the conclusion of the interview there is provision for me to sign your recommend; but mine is not the only important signature on your recommend. Before the recommend is valid, you must sign it yourself.' . . .

"And so it is. The Lord gives the privilege to members of the Church to respond to those questions in such interviews. Then if there is something amiss, the member can get his life in order so that he may qualify for the priesthood advancement, for a mission, or for a temple recommend." (*Ensign*, November 1978, pp. 41–42.)

As we strive for worthiness, a scripture we should not lose sight of is Doctrine and Covenants, section 136, verse 31: "He that will not bear chastisement is not worthy of [the Lord's] kingdom." Sometimes there is a great need for us to be chastised, disciplined, and corrected in a spirit of love, help, and hope. Guidance and suggestions should be offered in a loving way, but most of us have a tendency to rebel or be dismayed when someone suggests that our conduct is less than it should be. As Benjamin Franklin once said: "Those things that hurt, instruct. It is for this reason that wise people learn not to dread but to welcome problems."

In life there are requirements for almost all privileges. Education demands them; business has its regulations; sports and games have their rules; the Church has certain standards, and so on. But in every case there is help to meet those requirements. It is up to us to look for that assistance so we can understand the rules and strengthen ourselves as we receive direction from the sources available. It is not wise or proper for us to judge ourselves as being unworthy and thus stop our forward progress.

When we dwell on our own weaknesses, it is easy to dwell on feeling that we are unworthy. Somehow we need to bridge the gap between continually striving to improve and yet not feeling defeated when our actions aren't perfect all the time. We need to remove *unworthy* from our vocabulary and replace it with *hope* and *work*. This we can do if we turn to quieter, deeper, surer guidelines — the words of our prophets and leaders, past and present.

Abraham Lincoln wisely said, "It is difficult to make a man miserable while he feels he is worthy of himself and claims kindred to the great God who made him."

To reinforce the importance of the word *worthy* and worthy processes, I would like to share part of a poem by Elder Hugh B. Brown, entitled "I Would Be Worthy":

> I thank thee, Lord, that thou hast called me "son,"
> And fired my soul with the astounding thought
> That there is something of thee in me.

14

"I Would Be Worthy"

May the prophecy of this relationship
Impel me to be worthy.

I am grateful for a covenant birth;
For noble parents and an ancestry who beckon me
To heights beyond my grasp, but still attainable
If with stamina and effort I cultivate their seed
And prove that I am worthy.

I am grateful for a companion on this Eternal Quest,
Whose roots and birth and vision match my own;
Whose never-failing faith and loyalty have furnished light
        in darkness,
And re-steeled fortitude. May her faith in me
Inspire me to be worthy.

I am grateful for the lifting power of the gospel of thy Son;
For the knowledge thou hast given me of its beauty, truth and
        worth.
To attain its promised glory, may I to the end endure,
And then, forgiven, let charity tip the scales and allow me
To be considered worthy.[1]

I pray that we will learn individually and collectively the importance of the process of becoming worthy. We are entitled to the help of others not only in assessing our worthiness but also in making the classification of "worthy" available to each of us. As we measure our worthiness, let us no longer put limitations upon ourselves. Rather, let us use those strengths and powers that are available to make us worthy to gain great heights in personal development. Thus we will reap the joy that comes to those who desire to improve and who move forward with determination and effectiveness as they practice self-discipline and refuse to judge themselves as unworthy.

---

[1]*Eternal Quest*, Salt Lake City: Bookcraft, 1956, p. 13.

15

CHAPTER 3

"For There Are Many Gifts"

One of the great tragedies of life, it seems to me, is to describe oneself as having no talents or gifts. When, in disgust or discouragement, we allow ourselves to become despairing and depressed because of our self-appraisal, it is a sad day for us and a sad day in the eyes of God.

In the Doctrine and Covenants, we find this truth: "For all have not every gift given unto them; for there are many gifts, and to every man is given a gift by the Spirit of God. To some is given one, and to some is given another, that all may be profited thereby." (D&C 46:11–12.)

God has given each of us one or more special talents. Socrates made this famous statement: "The unexamined life is not worth living." It is up to each of us to search for and build upon the gifts God has given. We must remember that each of us is made in the image of God, and there are no unimportant persons. Everyone matters to God and to our fellow beings.

In the Book of Mormon, particularly 3 Nephi, chapters 11 through 26, when the Savior showed himself to the people on the American continent, many gifts are referred to as being very real and most useful. Taken at random, let me mention a few gifts that are not always evident or note-worthy but that are very important. Among these may be your gifts — gifts not so evident but nevertheless real and valuable.

Some of these less-conspicuous gifts are the gift of asking; the gift of listening; the gift of hearing and using a still, small voice; the gift of being able to weep; the gift of avoiding contention; the gift of being agreeable; the gift of avoiding vain repetition; the gift of seeking that which is righteous; the gift of not passing judgment; the gift of looking to God for guidance; the gift of being a disciple; the gift of caring for others; the gift of being able to ponder; the gift of offering prayer; the gift of bearing a mighty testimony; and the gift of receiving the Holy Ghost.

We must remember that to every person is given a gift by the Spirit of God. It is our right and responsibility to accept our gifts and to share them. God's gifts and powers are available to all.

1. *The Gift to Ponder*

As I study the scriptures, I am challenged and moved by the word *ponder,* which is used so frequently in the Book of Mormon. Dictionaries say that to *ponder* means to weigh mentally, think deeply about, deliberate, meditate.

When Jesus Christ came to teach the Nephites, he said, "Therefore, go ye unto your homes, and ponder upon the things which I have said, and ask of the Father, in my name, that ye may understand, and prepare your minds for the morrow, and I come unto you again." (3 Nephi 17:3.)

Through pondering, we give the Spirit an opportunity to impress and direct. Pondering is a powerful link between the heart and the mind. As we read the scriptures, our hearts and minds are touched. If we use the gift to ponder, we can take these eternal truths and come to realize how we can incorporate them into our daily actions.

Today, in response to President Ezra Taft Benson's encouragement, millions are reading the Book of Mormon, some for the first time, others as a regular habit. We must remind all that the fruits of this great book are the most beneficial when we ponder as we read. Pondering is a progressive mental pursuit. It is a great gift to those who learn to use it. We find understanding, insight, and practical application if we will use the gift of pondering.

2. The Gift to Look to God for Direction

How often have we ourselves said or have we heard others exclaim in times of crisis or trouble, "I just don't know where to turn"?

If we will just use it, a gift is available to all of us — the gift of looking to God for direction. Here is an avenue of strength, comfort, and guidance. The scriptures promise us: "Behold, I am the law, and the light. Look unto me, and endure to the end, and ye shall live; for unto him that endureth to the end will I give eternal life." (3 Nephi 15:9.) "Look to God and live." (Alma 37:47.)

If we look to God for guidance, what do we look for in his children that we may be profited thereby? Some seem to prefer the practice of looking for and pointing out the weaknesses of their associates. But it is the gifts others have, not their failings, that make it possible for all to profit thereby.

What a spiritual comfort and blessing it is to know that if we look to our Savior Jesus Christ and endure to the end, eternal life and exaltation can be ours. Our capacity to see and comprehend is increased only in proportion to our willingness to look. God becomes more approachable as we look to him. Looking to God teaches us to serve and live without compulsion. Being a leader in the Church should never diminish our looking-to-God time.

3. *The Gift to Hear and Use the Small Voice*

Still, small heavenly voices penetrate the heart with their gentle, convincing declarations: "And it came to pass that while they were thus conversing one with another, they heard a voice as if it came out of heaven; and they cast their eyes round about, for they understood not the voice which they heard; and it was not a harsh voice, neither was it a loud voice; nevertheless, and notwithstanding it being a small voice it did pierce them that did hear to the center, insomuch that there was no part of their frame that it did not cause to quake; yea, it did pierce them to the very soul, and did cause their hearts to burn." (3 Nephi 11:3.)

Hope, encouragement, and direction come most often from a soft, piercing voice. Small voices are heard only by those who are willing to listen. Soft and small voice communications with our associates make priceless friendships possible. I appreciate people who find no need to raise their voices as they try to impress or convince. Most people who argue and shout seem to have ceased listening to what the small voice could powerfully contribute.

We love the small voice of a child saying, "Mommy, Daddy, I love you."

How powerful is a small voice that knows how and when to say, "Thank you."

Think of the heavenly voice saying, "Joseph, this is my Beloved Son. Hear Him." (See Joseph Smith–History 1:17.)

19

It is heartwarming and reassuring to hear the small voice declare, "Be still, and know." (D&C 101:16.)

Remember that one of our greatest gifts is the small voice of the Holy Ghost whispering directions in our lives and making mighty testimonies possible.

4. The Gift to Calm

What a majestic gift it is to be able to calm others! We thank God for those who are calm instead of contentious. "He that hath the spirit of contention is not of me, but is of the devil, who is the father of contention, and he stirreth up the hearts of men to contend with anger, one with another." (3 Nephi 11:29.)

Contention is a tool of the adversary. Peace is a tool of our Savior. What a wonderful tribute we pay people when we describe them as being gentle, firm, and calm!

Contention stops progress. Love brings eternal progression. Where contention prevails, there can be no united effort in any purposeful direction.

"Cease to contend one with another; cease to speak evil one of another." (D&C 136:23.) Argument and debate must be supplanted by calm discussion, study, listening, and negotiation. The gospel teaches harmony, unity, and agreement. It must be presented in love, and with glad tidings, by those who are calm. We should learn to talk together, listen together, pray together, decide together, and avoid all forms of possible contention. We must learn to curb anger. Satan knows that when contention begins, orderly progress is thwarted.

There has never been a time when it is more important for us as members of The Church of Jesus Christ of Latter-day Saints to take a stand, remain firm in our convictions, and conduct ourselves with calm assurance under all circumstances. We must not be manipulated or enraged by those who subtly foster contention over issues of the day.

"Behold, this is not my doctrine, to stir up the hearts of men with anger, one against another; but this is my doctrine, that such things should be done away." (3 Nephi 11:30.) "Ye should live in peace one with another." (Mosiah 2:20.) Those with the gift of being calm make lasting peace possible.

5. The Gift to Care

How grateful we should be for families, friends, and organizations who care! They make life easier and more meaningful. They, too, reap rewards in their Christlike caring when they serve for the right reasons. Leaders on every level should be interested in rendering compassionate caring for others.

"And behold, I tell you these things that ye may learn wisdom; that ye may learn that when ye are in the service of your fellow beings ye are only in the service of your God." (Mosiah 2:17.)

Our Savior cares for all of his sheep. What a tribute it is to be recognized as one who cares. Let me share with you a story about the quiet caring of an unusual person.

Recently, during a twenty-fifth anniversary ward reunion in the Salt Lake Valley, a "Best Scouter Ever" award was presented. The special evening in the cultural hall, which included dinner as well as a fine program, drew many people back to the ward event because of the good feelings created over the past twenty-five years. The person acting as master of ceremonies introduced a young man to make this special award. He appeared to be about six feet four inches tall and well over two hundred pounds. He walked to the microphone and said, "We would now like to pay tribute to the best Scouter this ward has ever had."

Immediately names and faces of past Scout leaders jumped into the minds of those attending. Who would it be? There had been many great Scoutmasters in this ward. How could those in charge decide?

The tall, handsome young man mentioned many names of past Scout leaders and then said, "No, it is none of these, though they have all been great Scouters. Our ward 'Best Scouter Ever' award goes to someone who has worked in the Primary and as a Scout leader teaching boys for forty years. This individual has received the Silver Beaver Award, one of the highest awards given in Scouting, and the Silver Beehive Award, the highest award given by the Church in Scouting." Then with a voice that trembled slightly, he said, "Our 'Best Scouter Ever' recognition goes to Sister Jennie Verl Keefer." A hush came over the audience, then knowing voices of approval, then a burst of applause that seemed to go on forever.

Sister Keefer was called up to the front. All present intently watched her quietly make her way from the back of the room, her five-foot frame barely taller than those who were seated. Once at the microphone, the surprised recipient expressed a quiet and emotional, yet firm, thanks. She said between tears of gratitude that it hadn't been quite forty years she had served. It was only thirty-seven years. And then Sister Keefer proudly added that during all her time of service, she had never had a bad boy.

The presenter asked all those whom Sister Keefer had ever taught and cared for to come to the stage. Here was the amazing thing. Men and boys started from the audience and filled the space behind this tiny woman — doctors, bishops, presidents of companies, husbands, fathers holding babies, returned missionaries, contractors, computer workers, dentists, carpenters, and more. All these Scouts had as boys been touched by the service and caring of this one noble and great woman — the best Scouter ever in the ward's entire history. She had the gift of caring, and here were some of the fruits of her labors. Generations yet to come will bless her name for what she has done. What a great gift have those who know how to care!

"And to every man is given a gift." (D&C 46:11.) This is true. God does bless us with gifts. As we develop and share our God-given gifts and benefit from the gifts of those around us, the world can be a better place and God's work will move forward at a more rapid pace. May he help us to recognize, develop, and share our gifts, that all may profit thereby.

CHAPTER 4

"That's Just the Way I Am"

Almost a century ago, in an address on spiritual gifts, President George Q. Cannon said the following:

> No man ought to say, "Oh, I cannot help this; it is my nature." He is not justified in it, for the reason that God has promised to give strength to correct these things, and to give gifts that will eradicate them. If a man lack wisdom, it is his duty to ask God for wisdom. The same with everything else. That is the design of God concerning His Church. He wants His Saints to be perfected in the truth. For this purpose He gives these gifts, and bestows them upon those who seek after them, in order that they may be a perfect people upon the face of the earth, notwithstanding their many weaknesses, because God has promised to give the gifts that are necessary for their perfection.

In this memorable address, President Cannon also said:

> You have need to repent of your hardness of heart, of your indifference and of your carelessness. There is not that diligence, there is not that faith, there is not that seeking for the power of God that there should be among a people who have received the precious promises we have. Instead of the sick being healed, why, it is as much as you can do to get faith to believe that the administration of an elder will be attended with effect. There is not that seeking for the gift of healing and for the gift to be healed that there ought to be among the Saints. And so with other gifts and graces that God has placed

in His Church for His people. I say to you that it is our duty to avail ourselves of the privileges which God has placed within our reach. If we have done wrong, repent of our wrong and feel after God, and not be satisfied till we have found Him, and He hears and answers us, and He speaks by His divine power in our hearts, bearing testimony to us in such a manner as cannot be doubted that He hears us, that He is near to us, and that He is watching over us and ready to bestow upon us all the blessings that are necessary for our happiness here and hereafter.

If any of us are imperfect, it is our duty to pray for the gift that will make us perfect. Have I imperfections? I am full of them. What is my duty? To pray to God to give me the gifts that will correct these imperfections. If I am an angry man, it is my duty to pray for charity, which suffereth long and is kind. Am I an envious man? It is my duty to seek for charity, which envieth not. So with all the gifts of the Gospel. They are intended for this purpose. (November 26, 1893, reported in *Deseret Weekly* 48:33–34.)

This profound counsel comes from a man of great wisdom, and it is something that we today could beneficially accept as a standard. In today's world it would probably be spoken by some of us who are seeking to be comfortable with habits and shortcomings and would declare, "That's just the way I am." In some circles we would probably refer to this as a cop-out or a justification for not having the will or desire to improve ourselves by and through the gifts available to us through the truth found in the gospel of Jesus Christ.

I am disheartened and disturbed when I hear people avoiding the blessings and challenges of life by indicating to themselves, their associates, and their family, "I'm sorry, but that's just the way I am." This is an attitude that brings not only complacency but also a lack of progress. It is a prime cause of unhappiness.

How impressive it was in past years to hear President J. Reuben Clark, Jr., pray at a very advanced age for the Lord's assistance in helping him to continue and remain true and faithful to the end. Yes, to finish life's race with victory, and not resign himself to saying, "I'm in my nineties, and that's just the way I am."

How often we hear someone say, "I am just not cut out to be a leader in the Church. It's not my strength. It's not my way. I will attend and go as I feel impressed, but don't expect me to take positions of responsibility and leadership, because I am just not that way." With the gifts that are available from God, every one of us has the opportunity to be the beneficiary of gifts that will make our progress more meaningful and perfect.

It is dangerous for anyone to be lulled into lack of progress because "I just wasn't cut out to be a teacher," or "I wasn't cut out to be a good housekeeper," or "It's all right for other people to do these things, but it's impossible for me because it's just not my nature or strength."

No one has to be content with status quo. I've heard some of my friends who were having difficulty with drugs and alcohol say, "I guess I'm just supposed to be this way. My father was an alcoholic, and it comes natural for me to be the same." There are no reasons for failure and no traits of continuing downgrading just because an associate or family member has taken these routes in the course of life. We need to make up our minds we are going to take ourselves the way we are and, with God's help, add to our gifts and abilities.

It is unfair for us to label ourselves as saddled with this or that because we have failed to realize our potential and the spiritual gifts that are available as we pursue life's trails. It is true that everyone is given a gift. The gifts that are available to us for the benefit of all mankind are for self-improvement, self-development, and self-success so that we may be of value to our associates and those who need our strengths so badly.

I recall visiting at the Utah State Prison years ago during the summer time. As the warden and I visited in the outside recreational and exercise areas, I noticed that some of the men were not wearing shirts and were sweating in the heat. One prisoner who was shirtless had tattooed on his chest the words "A born loser." As I observed this, I thought that it was not too unusual to find someone with this kind of an attitude in prison. Perhaps he had convinced himself that prison was where he belonged, saying to himself, "That's just the way I am." He was conducting himself in such a manner that his stay in the prison would probably be lengthy because he had so identified himself.

Some of the strongest individuals I have met in life have been those who have partaken of spiritual gifts and have improved themselves, lifted themselves up, and become great despite environmental situations that might make it convenient to be comfortable in mediocrity or less.

The Master referred to spiritual gifts as "fruit" or "fruits." He said: "I am the vine, ye are the branches: He that abideth in me, and I in him, the same bringeth forth much fruit: for without me ye can do nothing. . . . Ye have not chosen me, but I have chosen you, and ordained you, that ye should go and bring forth fruit, and that your fruit should remain: that whatsoever ye shall ask of the Father in my name, he may give it you." (John 15:5, 16.)

27

In his memorable and powerful speech, President Cannon said: "How many of you, when you bow before your Heavenly Father in your family circle or in your secret places, contend for these gifts to be bestowed upon you? How many of you ask the Father, in the name of Jesus, to manifest Himself to you through these powers and these gifts? Or do you go along day by day like a door turning on its hinges, without having any feeling upon the subject, without exercising any faith whatever; content to be baptized and be members of the Church, and to rest there, thinking that your salvation is secure because you have done this? I say to you, in the name of the Lord, as one of His servants, that you have need to repent of this." (Ibid.)

How pleasing it is to witness unusual performance and to achieve outstanding levels of performance when conditions seem to have made it necessary for us to be average or losers because of surroundings, circumstances, or competition. We need to know how to motivate ourselves and others. I think of one of the greatest football coaches of all time. He wouldn't tolerate a losing attitude. He could often make his associates perform above and beyond their normal capacities. He had the gift of leadership. He wouldn't allow his team members to be down. Defeat was never part of the game plan.

I am impressed with the fact that God has made himself and others available to share these many gifts for our improvement and the benefit of the children of God. We are living in a day and a period of enlightenment when there is no time, reason, or occasion for anyone to justify labeling himself or herself with "I'm sorry — I'm doing the best I can under the circumstances." Often the limitations we place on ourselves are unfair, unreasonable, and unnecessary. Too often we hear people say, "Today is not my day," or "I'm one who is constantly unlucky." Too frequently we hear people excuse or justify their present situations with, "I just can't resist rich foods," "I know I find fault or criticize others constantly, but it's just part of my make-up," "It's difficult for me to keep a commitment. I don't seem to have the courage to stand firm when it really counts," "Being punctual is just impossible for me," or "I'm just not inclined to be friendly with others."

These are just a few examples of what we hear from those who would fault God for their lack of progress instead of loving him for his gifts that will help them to progress and attain happiness.

Miraculous powers are promised to those who will seek the gifts that are available from God, who humbly approach his throne continually for strength and powers above and beyond those that are natural to them. Those who approach their Heavenly Father with their needs will reap the benefits of spiritual gifts that can make the difference in their lives and the well-being of their associates.

We learn from section 46 of the Doctrine and Covenants some of the gifts available to give us guidance, strength, and the power for self-improvement on a daily basis. Think of the gift of being wise and having knowledge; the faith to be healed; the faith to heal; the spirit of discernment; the spirit to prophesy and to speak with tongues; the interpretation of tongues. What a glorious promise is in this section: "And it shall come to pass that he that asketh in Spirit shall receive in Spirit." (D&C 46:28.)

All of these spiritual opportunities are available to us

according to our needs and according to those things which are for our best good. How wonderful it is to contemplate that through the gift of the Holy Ghost we may declare in firmness and truth that Jesus is our Savior, our Lord, and our Messiah. When we testify by the Spirit, we not only grow individually, but we can also touch the lives of others who will recognize the source of testimony and confirming powers.

President Harold B. Lee once explained: "The Lord, by revelation, brings thought into our minds as though a voice were speaking. May I bear humble testimony to that fact? I was once in a situation where I needed help. The Lord knew I needed help, as I was on an important mission. I was awakened in the wee hours of the morning and was straightened out on something that I had planned to do in a contrary way, and the way was clearly mapped out before me as I lay there that morning, just as surely as though someone had sat on the edge of my bed and told me what to do. Yes, the voice of the Lord comes into our minds and we can be directed thereby." (*Stand Ye in Holy Places*, Salt Lake City: Deseret Book, 1974, p. 140.)

Consider also what President Joseph F. Smith said: "I believe that every individual in the Church has just as much right to enjoy the spirit of revelation and the understanding from God which that spirit of revelation gives him, for his own good, as the bishop has to enable him to preside over his ward." (*Gospel Doctrine*, Classics in Mormon Literature Series, Salt Lake City: Deseret Book, 1986, pp. 34–35.)

One of my favorite examples of someone who lifted himself by the spiritual gifts and strengths that were available is Joseph Smith, who said, "I am like a huge, rough stone rolling down from a high mountain; and the only polishing I get is when some corner gets rubbed off by coming in contact with something else, striking with accelerated force against religious bigotry, editors, suborned judges and jurors, and the authority of perjured executives, backed by mobs, blasphemers, licentious and corrupt men and women—all hell knocking off a corner here and a corner there. Thus I will become a smooth and polished shaft in the quiver of the Almighty." (*History of the Church* 5:401.)

Parley P. Pratt's report of the Prophet's conduct on a challenging night has always been one of my favorite examples of greatness and rising above circumstances:

> In one of those tedious nights we had lain as if in sleep till the hour of midnight had passed, and our ears and hearts had been pained, while we had listened for hours to the obscene jests, the horrid oaths, the dreadful blasphemies and filthy language of our guards, . . . as they recounted to each other their deeds of rapine, murder, robbery, etc., which they had committed among the "Mormons" while at Far West and vicinity. They even boasted of defiling by force wives, daughters and virgins, and of shooting or dashing out the brains of men, women and children.
>
> I had listened till I became so disgusted, shocked, horrified, and so filled with the spirit of indignant justice that I could scarcely refrain from rising upon my feet and rebuking the guards; but had said nothing to Joseph, or any one else, although I lay next to him and knew he was awake. On a sudden he arose to his feet, and spoke in a voice of thunder, or as the roaring lion, uttering, as near as I can recollect, the following words:
>
> "SILENCE, ye fiends of the infernal pit! In the name of Jesus Christ I rebuke you, and command you to be still; I will not live another minute and hear such language. Cease such talk, or you or I die THIS INSTANT!"
>
> He ceased to speak. He stood erect in terrible majesty. Chained, and without a weapon; calm, unruffled and dignified

31

as an angel, he looked down upon his quailing guards, whose weapons were lowered or dropped to the ground; whose knees smote together, and who, shrinking into a corner, or crouching at his feet, begged his pardon, and remained quiet until an exchange of guards.

I have seen ministers of justice, clothed in ministerial robes, and criminals arraigned before them, while life was suspended on a breath, in the Courts of England; I have witnessed a Congress in solemn session to give laws to nations; I have tried to conceive of kings, of royal courts, of thrones and crowns; and of emperors assembled to decide the fate of kingdoms; but dignity and majesty have I seen but *once,* as it stood in chains, at midnight, in a dungeon in an obscure village of Missouri. (*Autobiography of Parley P. Pratt,* Classics in Mormon Literature Series, Salt Lake City: Deseret Book, 1985, pp. 179–80.)

A great leader of young women, a person who spent a majority of her lifetime encouraging youth and youth leaders worldwide to constantly better themselves, was LaRue C. Longden, a former member of the Young Women's general presidency. Ponder her words: "For almost too many years to count, it has been my beautiful privilege to tell our precious young folks and their leaders that 'It is smart to be a Latter-day Saint.' As my parting shot, may I again reiterate, it is smart to be a Latter-day Saint, for to be one we are privileged to be baptized and confirmed by proper authority which brings us into our Father's kingdom. Then, through our young men, we women share in our Father's greatest gift to his children, his priesthood, through which our worthy men may act in his behalf. In a day of turmoil, false prophets, worry, supposed lack of security and decision, I want to say once more with a voice loud and clear, 'I am humbly grateful to be a Latter-day Saint, for I know it is truly smart to be a Latter-day Saint!' " (*It's Smart to Be a Latter-day Saint,* Salt Lake City: Deseret Book, 1967, p. 112.)

Sister Longden conveyed the message that in some parts of our society today it is considered smart to do many things that detract from a person's spirituality. Immodest fashions, sexual freedoms, use of drugs and narcotics, selfish mediocrity, and rebellion against sacred things seem to be typical of the times. During a lifetime of active service she found that smartness truly comes through espousing the standards of The Church of Jesus Christ of Latter-day Saints and carrying on regardless of peer pressure or conditions of the time.

Let us resolve this day that the phrase "that's just the way I am" will not be used as a crutch or excuse for lack of progress. Rather, let us use God's gifts and the example and strengths of others to live better today and hold on to principles that are eternal.

CHAPTER 5

A Pattern in All Things

Over the years I have experienced some uncomfortable times in commercial aircraft while traveling in turbulent skies. Oftentimes, heavy winds, storms, angry clouds, and downdrafts have caused bumpy and anxious moments, particularly when it was time to land. A seasoned pilot once gave me comfort after such an experience when he talked about a landing pattern — the ordered flight path of an aircraft about to touch down. Precise instruments, experience, and trust guide the planes to safety en route and through proper landing and takeoff. "We can't control the weather or elements, but we can stay within the pattern for safety," he emphasized.

One day I was admiring a beautiful hand-finished quilt made by a skilled seamstress. As we visited together, I learned that she had made many quilts over the years and was well known for her excellent handiwork. To my query, "Do you ever make one of these quilts without a pattern?" she said, "How would I know how it might turn out if I didn't have a pattern to follow?"

How can we even guess how our lives will turn out if we don't choose to follow the right pattern?

34

What a happy circumstance and strength in our day to have the Lord's promise, "I will give unto you a pattern in all things, that ye may not be deceived; for Satan is abroad in the land, and he goeth forth deceiving." (D&C 52:14.) I have always received courage, comfort, and direction from this powerful statement.

A pattern is a guide for copying, a design, a plan, a diagram or model to be followed in making things, a composite of traits or features characteristic of an individual. It is also the ordered flight path for an aircraft about to land.

The gospel of Jesus Christ is God's pattern for righteous living and eternal life. It makes possible goal setting and lofty priorities. Satan and his advocates will constantly try to deceive and entice us into following their patterns. If we are to achieve daily safety, exaltation, and eternal happiness, we need to live by the light and truth of our Savior's plan. All salvation revolves around our Savior.

I recently spoke with a drug addict about priorities, life's patterns, hopes, goals, and purposes. I was grieved when this attractive young woman said, "God is loving. God is kind. Leave me alone, and never mind." The wayward and disobedient will never be happy while smothered with Satan's suggestion that practice makes permanence. God's gift and commitment to agency will never include a tolerance of sin.

God is truly loving and kind. Part of his pattern is to help us use our gift of free agency, but his pattern does not condone sin. When we abuse our agency to choose a lifestyle contrary to revealed patterns, we must live with the consequences. If we are unwilling to follow the true and tested patterns given for our happiness, the result is heartache for us, for our families, and for our friends. Our freedom to choose our course of conduct does not provide personal freedom from the consequences of our performances. God's love for us is constant and will not diminish, but he cannot rescue us from the painful results that are caused by wrong choices.

It is no secret that Satan wages open war with the truth and with all those who live righteously. He deceives with skill and effectiveness even his own followers. He would have us give up, quit, and rebel when setbacks come. Sometimes when we are committed to and are following proper patterns, we experience heavy bumps and anxious hours. Many times true winners are those who have been hurt and disappointed but have risen above these challenges. Often God gives us difficulties to bring out the best in us. It is true that life does not determine winners. Winners determine life.

The great Olympic slogan says that the glory of the Olympic Games is not in the victory, but in taking part. Grantland Rice once wrote, "When the One Great Scorer comes to write against your name, he marks not that you won or lost, but how you played the game."

Satan has a way of wrapping enticing diversions with ribbons, bows, and fancy coverings. But inside are immorality, self-destruction, and substandard culture temptations. His established pattern is to deceive at all costs. "Live it up," "enjoy the 'now,' " "go for it," and "do your own thing" are some of his enticements for the susceptible in the days and hours to come. He cunningly uses deceit in its most dastardly form. He would have us forget that the essential thing in life is not in conquering, but in steadfast commitment to righteous patterns.

He is the author of all programs that dress up evil and wrong to whet our appetites. Yielding to temptations that promote immoral conduct will never bring happiness. When we are down and out and scrambling for relief from his clutches, he will continue to recommend patterns of conduct that allow us to destroy our self-respect.

Why does a loving God permit children he truly loves to be tempted by Satan and his ways? We have the answer from a great prophet: "Wherefore, the Lord God gave unto man that he should act for himself. Wherefore, man could not act for himself save it should be that he was enticed by the one or the other." (2 Nephi 2:16.)

We must avoid Satan's territory of deceit. It will never lead to happiness. Evidence to the contrary, there are no successful sinners. All of us must one day stand before God and be judged according to our personal deeds done in the flesh. The burdens of the sinner will never be lighter than those of the saint. Be not deceived by the lures of Satan. God is at the helm and is grieved when we, his children, stray from proven paths of enduring happiness and righteousness. He would have us hold fast to the iron rod with total commitment and strength.

One of Satan's most intriguing traps among many of God's children today seems to be a trend to postpone taking on mature personal responsibilities, such as avoiding marriage because of the possibility of divorce, and becoming involved in the drug culture because life is so uncertain. There are segments of our population that march, protest, and demand handouts and cures rather than follow God's rules of prevention and self-discipline. Following revealed patterns helps us to recognize our weaknesses, deal positively with them, overcome them, and rise to Christlike heights.

We must, if we will have happiness, follow the straight and prescribed paths. "I will give you a pattern in all things" is one of the Lord's greatest gifts and promises. If we keep our minds occupied with constructive, useful things on a constant basis, Satan will not have success in idle minds. Good music, art, literature, recreation, and other worthy pastimes can help establish proper patterns in our minds and conduct. Happiness is a by-product of righteous living and sharing within the framework of lofty patterns. Actions of the moment may be fun, but true happiness depends upon how we feel after the involvement is over.

Besides patterns for prayer, we have direction for pondering, procedure, patience, action, and integrity. There are patterns for all worthy things if we will search for them. "And behold, it must be done according to the pattern which I have given unto you." (D&C 94:2.) There is no other proven way. "And again, he that is overcome and bringeth not forth fruits, even according to this pattern, is not of me. Wherefore, by this pattern ye shall know the spirits in all cases under the whole heavens." (D&C 52:18–19.)

In all phases of life, it is expedient that we have correct patterns to follow.

One of my favorite sports stories has to do with Roger Bannister, who many years ago participated in the Olympic Games in the one-mile race. He was supposed to win, but he wound up finishing in fourth place. He went home from the Olympics discouraged, disillusioned, and embarrassed.

His mind was set on giving up running. He was a medical student at the time, and he decided that he'd better get on with life and devote all of his time to preparing for medicine and forget his hopes about setting a world record for the mile. He went to his coach and told him, "Coach, I'm through. I'm going to devote all my time to studying." His coach said, "Roger, I think you are the man who can break the four-minute mile. I wish you'd give it one last try before you quit." Roger didn't answer. He went home not knowing what to say or to do. But before the night was over, he had convinced himself that he would develop an iron will before he quit running. He was going to break the four-minute mile.

He knew what this meant. He would have to set a pattern and live by it. He realized he would have to study seven, eight, or even nine hours a day to get through medical school. He would have to train for at least four hours a day. Also involved was running consistently to build up his body to the peak of perfection. He knew he would have to eat the best foods. He knew he would have to go to bed early every night and sleep nine or ten hours, to let his body recuperate and constantly build up for the great day. He determined that he was going to follow the rigid pattern that he and the coach knew was necessary for victory and achievement.

On May 6, 1954, Roger Bannister—a tall, stooped Englishman with a big-boned, angular face and a ruddy complexion, a man committed to winning—broke the four-minute mile barrier. On a dreary, wet, windy day, he went to the Oxford University track to put his theories and skill to the test. His parents and a few hundred others were present. The rest is history. Running strictly according to his charts and pattern, he ran the miracle mile in 3:59.4. He became the first man in recorded history to speed across this distance in less than four minutes. He proved that man could run faster than was thought possible. He paid the price and reaped the rewards of following the proper pattern, and as a result he became an international hero in all the record books. The four-minute-mile barrier is broken frequently these days, but Roger Bannister set the pattern many years ago and followed it with total commitment, self-discipline, and a will of iron.

Patterns are given by the Lord so that we may follow, reason, and endure in righteousness. Within the Church is an established pattern for receiving revelation and instructions. We need to be reminded that anyone claiming to receive direction or revelation for others should be held suspect. This is especially true when the content is believed to have relevance for areas, regions, stakes, or wards in the Church for whom the person has no particular responsibility. God reveals his will through his prophets today as he did in the past.

Our Savior, Jesus Christ, established a pattern of conduct for all mankind. He reminded us, "If ye love me, feed my sheep." (John 21:17.) The love is greater than the who, where, how, or when. It must be unconditional and constant.

To gain exaltation and happy daily life, we must follow a pattern of righteousness. Our self-esteem and success can best be measured by how we follow the patterns of life in avoiding deceit, haughtiness, pride, or pessimism. Solid, permanent progress can take place only if deception is avoided, no matter how advantageous it may seem to yield or compromise basic principles of conduct.

Be not deceived. God is not mocked. He knows what is best for his children, for those who love him and develop the traits and characteristics shown by his Only Begotten Son, Jesus Christ. "For behold, it is not meet that I should command in all things," he has told us, "for he that is compelled in all things, the same is a slothful and not a wise servant; wherefore he receiveth no reward." (D&C 58:26.)

Instead of our being commanded in all things, we are given a *pattern* in all things. The choice to use the safe paths is ours. May God help us to follow his patterns and reap the rewards he has in store for the obedient.

CHAPTER 6

Lessons from the Master

For as long as I can remember I've had a special love
for Jesus Christ. I was taught that he is the Son of the
Living God. I was taught that he is my friend, my teacher,
and my strength. Through the years, when the calling and
responsibility and honor of bearing special witness of him
have come into my life, I have endeavored to be taught by
his life and his ways. Truly, he is the Master Teacher. To
assist me in my labors and commitment, I have found myself
turning frequently to the eighth chapter of John in the New
Testament for strength, for guidance, and for example.

> Jesus went unto the Mount of Olives. And early in the
> morning he came again into the temple, and all the people
> came unto him; and he sat down, and taught them. And the
> scribes and Pharisees brought unto him a woman taken in
> adultery; and when they had set her in the midst,
> They say unto him, Master, this woman was taken in adul-
> tery, in the very act. Now Moses in the law commanded us,
> that such should be stoned: but what sayest thou?
> This they said, tempting him, that they might have to accuse
> him. But Jesus stooped down, and with his finger wrote on the
> ground, as though he heard them not. So when they continued
> asking him, he lifted up himself, and said unto them, He that
> is without sin among you, let him first cast a stone at her.
> And again he stooped down, and wrote on the ground.

42

And they which heard it, being convicted by their own conscience, went out one by one, beginning at the eldest, even unto the last: and Jesus was left alone, and the woman standing in the midst.

When Jesus had lifted up himself, and saw none but the woman, he said unto her, Woman, where are those thine accusers? hath no man condemned thee?

She said, No man, Lord. And Jesus said unto her, Neither do I condemn thee: go, and sin no more.

Then spake Jesus again unto them, saying, I am the light of the world: he that followeth me shall not walk in darkness, but shall have the light of life. (John 8:1-12.)

Let us examine some of the words in this passage of scripture to strengthen our lives and our relationships with Jesus. These lines and words help me to better understand him and give me the desire to do and be more like him.

The first word: Jesus. I love the word *Jesus*. I love Jesus of Nazareth. It troubles me when I hear this sacred name used in vain. We must not allow ourselves to speak this word without reverence. Even though it is the world's way today to use that name in exclamation, in failure, to get attention, and to curse, let us not allow ourselves to use the name of Jesus without reverence.

I like the second word, *went*. I learn from it that Jesus wasn't carried; he wasn't picked up; he wasn't conveyed. He *went*. He was self-motivated, self-disciplined. I love that word *went*. He sought privacy, seclusion for meditation in the Mount of Olives, where he could ponder and pray and prepare. Early in the morning he was about his Father's business.

Early one morning my telephone rang in the Church Administration Building. It was a little before seven in the morning, and the familiar voice of President Spencer W.

Kimball — weak, but powerful — said, "Marvin, could I come up to your office and see you?" I said, "President Kimball, if you want to see me I'll be right down." He said, "Would you do that?" I was down in his office in thirty seconds. He handed me a letter and said, "Would you read this and tell me what you think?" I suppose he did this with a lot of us — asking for our opinion. My opinion isn't that special. I read it and said, "President Kimball, you might want to think about doing it this way." And, bless his heart, he said, "That's what I thought and that's what we'll do." I went back to my office and felt fear and trembling for the rest of the day.

President Ezra Taft Benson knows how to work, and he starts early. Early in his life he learned to pray, work, and study. Early one morning he too phoned. His greeting was, "Marv, I knew you'd be there."

From these beloved prophets I have learned that we must be early and get a good start.

In the passage from John, we learn that Jesus "came again into the temple." It was a habit. It was a regular way for him to act, a way of life. And "all the people came unto him." He attracted people. All came. He was personable, wise, and kind, and they were attracted to him. But not all were converted. Some remained enemies. Some remained bitter. Others were taught.

In John's beautiful scripture that I love so much and am inclined to use as a guideline for my personal use, we learn that Jesus "sat down, and taught them." He didn't talk down to the people. He didn't talk up. He spoke to them as friends. He taught on the mount, along the road, in the marketplace, in a boat, or on the shores — wherever and whenever he was. He sat down and taught the people. He didn't threaten. He didn't scold. He didn't belittle. He humbly showed the way with parables, kindness, and great wisdom. Certainly he was not a scribe. He was the Son of God. He taught eye to eye, person to person, heart to heart. He sat down.

I once had the opportunity of sitting down with a prophet in an unusual circumstance. It is something I shall never forget. President Kimball called me one day and said, "I'd like to go to the Utah State Prison and visit for a limited time." Without going into detail, I think that the thing that prompted his request and his motivation was something as simple as pure religion — going undefiled before God to visit the fatherless, the downtrodden, the weary, the prisoners. So we went to the Utah State Prison. He wanted to shake hands with a few, visit for a while, and then return to his office.

When we arrived at the institution, the warden had arranged to have two prisoners in his office. One had been convicted of murder and the other of grand larceny. One was a member of the Church and the other a nonmember. The warden and I waited to see what President Kimball would do. What would he say? He could have said, "I'm sure ashamed of you two. What did you do to get here? How many times have you been here before?" But he didn't.

President Kimball looked intently at one of the men, who hadn't even raised his eyes off the floor, and kept looking at him. Finally the man looked up, and President Kimball said, "Tell me about your mother." The prisoner spoke about his mother. And when that was over, President Kimball looked at the other one and asked, "What does your father

45

do?" I will never forget that moment. Instead of saying, "You big dummy, you should have known better than that," President Kimball said, "What does your father do?" I was taught by a prophet. I saw a prophet with a Christlike approach.

In the scripture, scribes and Pharisees brought to Jesus "a woman taken in adultery." Those enemies who would disturb, embarrass, ridicule, and display their cunningness — they tried to trick him. They sat the woman in the midst of the people as an exhibit, as a sinner, as someone unclean. But Jesus didn't flee from her presence. I feel close to that situation in which the scribes and Pharisees approached him and called him "Master," as if to say, "You who have all the answers, tell us." They probed. They were unreasonable. This woman had been taken in adultery — in the very act. There was no doubt about her guilt. They were setting Jesus up in what appeared to be an impossible situation.

The law of Moses said the woman should be stoned. "What sayest thou?" the scribes and Pharisees asked, tempting Jesus, trapping him, putting him in a no-win position. Whatever he said, he would be accused of wrong-doing, wrong judgment. They were tempting him to see if they could get him to lose his patience and forget who he was. Stoning her would be cruel. Ignoring her would be wrong. Asking her to leave would be beneath him. He stooped down and wrote on the ground as though he did not hear them, thus getting their attention and preparing everyone within earshot to be taught. We don't know what he wrote on the ground with his finger. For our purposes here, we'll say he was getting their attention while ignoring their cries for action and response. I can hear their questions of mischief: "C'mon, say something. We've got you. Are you afraid to answer?" But Jesus was in charge. Soon this would be evident, but his silence had to go on a little longer. Then he "lifted up himself," in humble and meek majesty, and said these most powerful words: "He that is without sin among you, let him first cast a stone at her." A perfect answer from a perfect person.

Today in our responsibilities, situations, and callings, we need to be reminded of this over and over again. In our dealings with all people, let the person who is without sin be the first to criticize, find fault, or belittle, or be the first to stone someone's character. When Jesus stooped down and wrote again on the ground, the people felt the impact of his silence while he said nothing. Convicted by their own consciences, they left on their own, not driven away. They went out one by one — not to find stones, but to nurse their spiritual wounds.

Jesus was left alone with the woman. I'm glad that's recorded. Some of us are inclined to avoid being with those who have fallen — they're beneath or below us. Left alone with the woman, Jesus said, "Where are those thine accusers? Hath no man condemned thee?" He was involving her in the interview and teaching at the same time. He took time to ask and to listen. Oh, if we could do more of that! Our answers would be so much easier, so much improved.

A few years ago a stake president called and said, "I haven't been able to resolve a certain situation. Would you be good enough to help me?" I arranged a time and met with a young man from Brigham Young University — 265 pounds, an all-conference tackle — and his parents. The

47

young man was a sophomore with two more years of football to play. His mother thought it would be nice if he played football, but his father wanted him to go on a mission. The more interviews there were, the more confusion there was.

After the usual greetings, I looked at the mother and said, "Do I understand that you favor your son's playing football?" She said, "Yes, I think I lean in that direction." I looked at the father and said, "Am I right in assuming you would like to have your son go on a mission at this time?" He said, "Yes, I lean in that direction." Then I looked at the football player and said, "What would *you* like to do?" He said, "I'd like to go on a mission." I said, "Why don't you?"

The interview was over and he went on a mission. I love this kind of situation! How much fun I could have had if I had spent a half hour arguing about which comes first and when, how, and where.

The woman taken in adultery answered the Lord's question regarding her accusers by saying, "No man, Lord." And then came this powerful declaration: "Go, and sin no more." The Master was teaching in that day, and he is also teaching in ours. His great message: Despise the sin but love the sinner. He did not condone adultery. He gave the woman love instead of a lecture. She and the accusers needed a lesson in love. The situation called for mercy and compassion. How rewarding it is to know that Jesus believed that man is greater than all of his sins. Is it any wonder he was referred to as the "Good Shepherd"? He loved all of his sheep whether they were strays, hungry, helpless, cold, or lost.

At the conclusion of this great teaching experience in

John, this lesson of love and compassion, is an important verse: "Then spake Jesus again unto them, saying, I am the light of the world: he that followeth me shall not walk in darkness, but shall have the light of life." (John 8:12.)

Let us follow his light. Let us refer often to these few words. I bear witness that they were preserved for the good of everyone in our day. We shall not walk in darkness, but shall have the light of life.

Later on in this same chapter of John, after the Pharisees had been with the Savior and were confounded, confused, impressed, and touched, they were heard to say, "Who art thou?" And his simple answer was, "The same that I said unto you from the beginning." (John 8:25.)

Recall Peter's answer when Jesus asked, "Whom do men say that I the Son of man am?" The disciples replied, "Some say that thou art John the Baptist: some, Elias; and others, Jeremias, or one of the prophets." Then Jesus asked, "But whom say ye that I am?"

Peter answered, "Thou art the Christ, the Son of the living God."

Then Jesus said, "Blessed art thou, Simon Bar-jona: for flesh and blood hath not revealed it unto thee, but my Father which is in heaven. And I say also unto thee, That thou art Peter, and upon this rock I will build my church; and the gates of hell shall not prevail against it." (Matthew 16:13–18.)

Let us have our answer when the question "Who art thou?" comes to us or pops up in our minds. Let us know with each passing day who he is and live closer to him.

Another of my favorite verses is also in the eighth chapter of John. After this series of teachings and experiences,

49

with people asking who he was and what was his purpose, trying to trick him and embarrass him, I suppose Jesus came to the point where he thought, *What do I have left to say to them? My life and my ways don't seem to affect them.* In verse twenty-six, at the climax of this story, he said, "He that sent me is true." (John 8:26.)

Jesus Christ was bearing his testimony that God is real and that his ways are true and right. When we don't seem to have all the answers and we are not very effective in communicating the feelings of our hearts through words, we should go to the scriptures. A testimony is a priceless possession, and it is peculiar and valuable to all members of The Church of Jesus Christ of Latter-day Saints. Jesus gave us the pattern. When all other channels seemed to be plugged with poisonous prejudice, he bore his testimony.

God the Father has not left us alone. When we do the things that please him, we will have joy in him and in ourselves. He has told us, through his Son, "If ye continue in my word, then are ye my disciples indeed; and ye shall know the truth, and the truth shall make you free." (John 8:31-32.)

I love that word *continue*. If we continue, we are his disciples. We may not all be called to positions of heavy and mighty responsibility, but we can have satisfaction in knowing that the final test is "Are you continuing in my word, and will you continue?"

The family, the home, the continuing make us disciples—not titles or honors. Not only may we know Jesus Christ as the Master Teacher, our Redeemer, Savior, and the Only Begotten of the Father, but we may know him in ways that touch our souls and give us daily direction, for he is the light and the way.

50

CHAPTER 7

"I Will Not Boast of Myself"

When I was a boy, I liked to hear about King Arthur. In the story of King Arthur, Queen Guinevere gives this advice to Lancelot, the bravest of the Knights of the Round Table: "For I would not have you declare yourself to the world until you have proved your worthiness. Wherefore do not yourself proclaim your name, but wait until the world proclaimeth it."

How much more effective it is in our day also to let the world see our good works rather than to hear us dwell on our own accomplishments or point out our impressive achievements.

We should remember to avoid the damaging effects that can come when we appear to be boasting about increased numbers or growth. How much better it is to let others measure our achievements rather than misunderstand as we recite on a continuing basis our percentages, progress, or family performances.

To boast means to glorify oneself, to talk in a vain or bragging manner, or to talk especially about one's deeds. To boast is to speak with pride and to take pride in, to brag about, to be proud to possess. Oftentimes, boastful people

51

are starving for attention. Boastful people may not be aware of the consequences caused by their method of presentation.

In the Book of Mormon, Ammon gives us excellent guidelines for putting our success in proper perspective. When Ammon's brother Aaron rebuked him, saying: "Ammon, I fear that thy joy doth carry thee away unto boasting," Ammon replied, "I do not boast in my own strength, nor in my own wisdom; but behold, my joy is full, yea, my heart is brim with joy, and I will rejoice in my God. Yea, I know that I am nothing; as to my strength I am weak; therefore I will not boast of myself, but I will boast of my God, for in his strength I can do all things; yea, behold, many mighty miracles we have wrought in this land, for which we will praise his name forever." (Alma 26:10–12.)

We can be much more effective in our conversations and conduct if we avoid the demeaning effect of boasting. We should let others become aware of our accomplishments by observation rather than by our boasting or flaunting them before the world. Boasting diminishes credibility and too often alienates friends, family members, and even those who may observe us from a distance.

We are humbly grateful for the increased number of conversions, for the many missionaries in the field, and for the evidence of improved commitments to and in the Church. However, we might well recall the response of Spencer W. Kimball when he was told of the great numbers of missionaries serving in the field. He said, "I am thankful, but not impressed." He expressed gratitude, but he also urged us to refrain from basking in their glory and to move on to higher levels and new horizons. Our Savior, Jesus Christ, to whose church we belong, would be disappointed if we ever created the impression that the efforts and the hard work put forth to build his kingdom were based only on the wisdom and power of man.

Recently at a women's conference, a speaker told about how he had been successful in land development and how everything he had touched had turned to gold. He had also tried to live a faithful life and had been an active servant in the gospel. Eventually he was called as a mission president. After a very effective mission, he had subsequently returned home. Then a combination of changing interest rates and other business factors caused his once-prosperous business to plummet. In fact, he lost nearly everything.

Telling the story, this man said, "I realized that I'd become quite boastful — that while I felt I had a testimony of Jesus Christ, in my mind I had brought about all of these wonderful things through my hard work, intelligence, and so forth. But when hard times hit, I began to realize how offensive I must have been to others and to my Heavenly Father to assume that I had brought all of these good things on my own. I felt like I'd lived a life of arrogance and boasting."

Helaman's advice to his sons Nephi and Lehi can give us strength today: "Therefore, my sons, I would that ye should do that which is good. . . . And now my sons, behold I have somewhat more to desire of you, which desire is, that ye may not do these things that ye may boast, but that ye may do these things to lay up for yourselves a treasure in heaven, yea, which is eternal." (Helaman 5:7–8.) Helaman wanted his sons to do good for the right reasons — not to boast, but to lay up treasures in heaven.

"Let not thy left hand know what thy right hand doeth"

is counsel often stated. (Matthew 6:3.) This is especially true when we have the opportunity to comfort, console, or counsel any who are confused, troubled, or weary. Whatever success we might have as we try to help should usually not be discussed, let alone boasted about. Humble, quiet, compassionate service is soul-rewarding. Why would one need to point out the subject or location of kindly deeds?

"For although a man may have many revelations, and have power to do many mighty works, yet if he boasts in his own strength, and sets at naught the counsels of God, and follows after the dictates of his own will and carnal desires, he must fall and incur the vengeance of a just God upon him." (D&C 3:4.)

How easy it is for people to believe that temporal success has been achieved by their own skills and labor. Everything good comes from the Lord.

Consideration for the feelings of others should always be important to worthy Latter-day Saints. Rightfully we may be happy about the number of children with which we have been blessed, the missionaries who have served, the temple marriages of our offspring, and the accomplishments of family members. However, others who are not so fortunate may have feelings of guilt or inadequacy. They may have been praying long and hard for the same blessings about which we are boasting, and they may feel that they are out of favor with God.

For this reason our appreciation should be sincerely felt, and we should express gratitude frequently to our Father in Heaven—but not too vocally to the world. We should be gratefully aware of the source of our blessings and strengths and refrain from taking undue credit for personal accomplishments.

When we dwell on where we have been, where we are now, and what we have now spiritually or financially, we may create resentment rather than respect. Boasting, whether it be done innocently or otherwise, is not good. Too frequently it creates an impression of more interest in self than in others.

Over the years, as a participant in team athletics, I have observed that often the star performer who boasts of his achievements and records asks for trouble. Those whose records are truly impressive are those who acknowledge the strengths of teammates, coaches, and managers and who thank God himself for their talents and abilities. Opponents in athletic competitions seem to lie in wait to clobber those who boast in their own strength.

God is pleased when we humbly recognize his powers and his influence in our accomplishments rather than indicate by words or innuendo that we have been responsible for remarkable achievements.

We learn from James 3:5 that often "the tongue is a little member, and boasteth great things." No thinking persons will permit their comments, attitudes, or expressions to be construed as boasting in their own strength. Those who persist in boasting fail to recognize the true sources of personal achievement.

History teaches us that those who boast in their own strength cannot have lasting success. We should be reminded constantly that we must not boast of faith nor of mighty works, but instead should boast of God in his blessings and goodness to us. He will help us to understand that humility must be our foundation if his goodness is to continue to come to and from us. Those who boast will certainly fall, because in their own strength no one endures. Those who boast or are conceited are not expected by their peers to achieve great heights, because they convey an attitude that they are already there.

One of the most common of all sins among worldly people is relying on and then boasting in the arm of the flesh. This is a most serious evil. It is a sin born of pride, a sin that creates a frame of mind that keeps people from turning to the Lord and accepting his saving grace. When individuals knowingly or unknowingly engage in self-exultation because of their riches, political power, worldly learning, physical prowess, business ability, or even works of righteousness, they are not in tune with the Spirit of the Lord.

We would all do well to take a lesson from the Savior, who repeatedly acknowledged and gave credit to the Father in all things. Indeed, that precedent was set in the premortal council when Jesus Christ pledged the fruits of all he might himself accomplish to go to the Father: "And the glory be thine forever." (Moses 4:2.)

During his mortal ministry, Jesus raised Jairus's daughter to life. "And her parents were astonished," Luke says, as well they should have been, "but he charged them that they should tell no man." (Luke 8:56.) Mark's account says, "he charged them straitly that no man should know it." (Mark 5:43.)

This wondrous deed that turned death into life, that bore record of the divinity of the One who even now was forecasting his own future victory over the grave, and that could be performed only in righteousness and only by the power of God—this mighty miracle should, as Matthew says, send Jesus' fame into all the land on its own merits. (See Matthew 4:24.)

Indeed, the parents of the young women could not enshroud in secrecy what was already public knowledge. Because of the way Jesus himself had handled the successive events, everyone in the whole area would soon know that the girl who once was dead now lived. Her death had been announced openly to the multitude. Jesus himself had replied before the multitude that, notwithstanding her death, she would "be made whole." (Luke 8:50.) All the people would soon know that she now lived, and they could only be expected to wonder how and by what means life had come to her again. Though the parents were charged to "tell no man," they told of this wondrous event to outsiders who were aware of the miracle.

We counsel and encourage those who enjoy the gifts of the Spirit and who possess the signs that follow those who believe that they must not boast of these spiritual blessings. In our day, after naming the miraculous signs that always attend those who have faith and those who believe the very truth taught by Jesus anciently, the Lord has said: "But a commandment I give unto them, that they shall not boast themselves of these things, neither speak them before the world; for these things are given unto you for your profit and for salvation." (D&C 84:73.)

Perhaps Jesus' charge to "tell no man" meant that Jairus's family were not to tell the account in a boastful way, lest a spirit of pride — a spirit of self-adopted superiority — should come into their souls. There were times when Jesus told the recipients of his healing power to go forth and testify of the goodness of God unto them, and other times when he limited the extent and detail of their witness.

57

The many admonitions in the scriptures to avoid boasting send the message that we should realize the source of all our blessings. Everything is given by God. All talents, creativity, ability, insight, and strength come from him. In our own strength we can do nothing, as Ammon admitted to his brother. When we seek the praise of man more than the praise of God, it will become easy to fall. But when we seek the Lord's help and thank him for all that we have and are, boasting will be erased.

God help us to humbly accept his blessings of strength and guidance. The wise and committed will praise his name forever and will avoid the very appearance of any attitudes or situations that feature personal accomplishments or boastings.

CHAPTER 8

How Much Attention Is Fair?

Much attention in our day is given to superstar athletes, movie stars, the beautiful people, the most intelligent, the best singers, the greatest entertainers, and so forth. This is just part of life. It isn't the way of life. People should be recognized. We should be recognized for our achievements, not our popularity.

As we look at ourselves and wonder if we're achieving or accomplishing, we must remember one thing. We should never compare ourselves with others. We should be concerned only about our own personal records and achievements, the strides we make in a particular field or the strides we make in our assignments in the Church, the improvement we make, and how we are progressing according to our own measurement. As one bishop told his congregation, "Many people compare apples and oranges and then go bananas over the statistics."

It is not good to compare ourselves to the Albert Einsteins, the Elizabeth Taylors, the Bo Dereks, and the John McEnroes of this world. We may go bananas over the results. What we must do is take note of our own personal growth and try to improve each day. The scriptures tell us, "The

59

glory of God is intelligence." This does not mean that God glories in those of us who are the most intelligent. It does mean we have to strive to learn something new each day. It means we have to read good books, stretch ourselves, and improve ourselves. That's what the glory of God is — what we do with the intelligence we have, what we do to stretch ourselves and improve ourselves.

So how much attention is fair? Let me give you some examples. A few years ago at a Brigham Young University football game, I observed as the homecoming queen and two attendants were introduced at halftime. They rode around the stadium seated in a red convertible. The weather was beautiful, and approximately 60,000 people were in attendance. According to the announcer, the royalty were selected for their beauty, talent, and poise. They were honored. They were quoted. They were crowned. Now I am not opposed to beauty queen contests and I am not talking about the merits of such recognition, but I am trying to put over a point. How much attention is fair? How much attention is good? What is fair to the person? Do we do others a favor when we give them too much attention?

That Saturday afternoon at the football game, a special award was presented to a young man by the name of Dale Murphy. At that time he was a baseball star for the Atlanta Braves. A convert to the Church and a former BYU student, he had been named the outstanding player in the National League.

I am proud of Dale Murphy. I saw him at half-time and we visited. I don't know what happened during the first half as far as he was concerned, but I know he didn't see any of the second half of the game. Everybody wanted to talk to him. Everyone wanted to corner him. And as I saw him walking around with his wife, never having a chance to look out at the game, this question came to my mind again. How much attention is fair? How much is right? How much is good?

For some reason people like to pay attention to those who are prominent and famous, and to tell their friends that they know them or saw them and talked to them. While I was talking to Dale's wife, somebody else had pulled him away. She told me, "During the week we went to the Atlanta Temple. I thought no one but our bishop and stake president knew we were going there. But when we arrived, a lot of people were standing in front of the temple wanting Dale to sign autographs and shake their hands." She also said that when others found out they were in the temple, they lined up afterwards to get the chance to visit. How much attention is fair?

I might add that one of the things I like about going to the temple is that we all dress the same. We don't know who is sitting next to us. We don't know who is in front or in back. There is no rank. We are all brothers and sisters, and we can sit together in meditation and worship. How much attention is fair? How much is good? How much is right?

So that Saturday, after visiting with the Murphys, I was a little disappointed and, I might say, also a little pleased that I am not Dale Murphy. I am very pleased that Dale Murphy is a national hero and active in the Church, but I still want the right to ask the question, How much attention is fair?

Some time ago I received a thought-provoking letter

from a young woman who said, "I love this gospel. But I do not enjoy being single and classified as such. I'm still the same person and don't need a special group for just singles. In Relief Society we're having a lesson titled 'The Single Parent.' How hard it will be to sit through that lesson. Why do we need a special lesson talking about the single parent? It's hard enough anyway, so why do I always have to be made different? Aren't we all brothers and sisters together in this church, working to help each other? I don't see special groups and lessons for people in other situations. And I know I speak for others, not just myself. Yes, the singles do have special needs, but so do others. Every time I sit in a singles meeting, I want to just scream out 'I'm not different.' "

The same may be true of people who have physical handicaps. I am sure they do not like to be treated as if they are different from everyone else. They want to be treated just like everyone else. They don't want to be singled out because of their differences, just as the woman who is divorced does not want to be singled out because she is a single parent. Again I ask, How much attention is fair? How much is right? How much is good?

I know a man who has lost one of his hands. I hear some people refer to him as "the man with the one hand." I am not so sure he would be pleased if he knew he was identified that way. He is a wonderful leader, and I am sure he would not like to be referred to as someone who has a physical deficiency that is visible. I take comfort in the fact that we all have weaknesses. Some of them are physical; some are emotional; some are mental; and some are spiritual. But we don't have to be labeled. How much attention is fair?

The scriptures tell us, "The worth of souls is great in the sight of God." (D&C 18:10.) I believe with all my heart that a soul is greater than a superstar. I wish that we could remember this and believe it and have a greater self-image. We have the opportunity to be of great worth because we are souls.

In Matthew we read: "At the same time came the disciples unto Jesus, saying, Who is the greatest in the kingdom of heaven?" In other words, "Who is the superstar? Who is the greatest? Tell us so we can copy them."

"And Jesus called a little child unto him, and set him in the midst of them, And said, Verily I say unto you, Except ye be converted, and become as little children, ye shall not enter into the kingdom of heaven. Whosoever therefore shall humble himself as this little child, the same is greatest in the kingdom of heaven. And whoso shall receive one such little child in my name receiveth me.

"But whoso shall offend one of these little ones [who would offend one of these little ones by giving him too much attention—or not enough] it were better for him that a millstone were hanged about his neck, and that he were drowned in the depth of the sea." (Matthew 18:1–6.)

Humility. Conversion. Innocence. All these virtues and attributes of a child make us the greatest. I am disappointed in people who like to drop names and say they know so-and-so and spend time with them. I like the statement that you can judge people by the way they treat those who can do them no earthly good or give them no earthly advantage.

Some of us are set on receiving the popular, the talented, the wealthy, and the famous rather than the lonely, the widow, the fatherless, or the afflicted. Whom did the Savior single out? Who was the greatest? How important is humility? How important is self-pride? How important is self-improvement?

Let me share another example on this subject, a story that was told by Elder Matthew Cowley, a great apostle with special warmth and heart. Elder Cowley said that he was in Canada one weekend for a conference and was invited to the home of one of the bishops for dinner. The bishop indicated that he would have liked to have had Elder Cowley stay in his home, but he didn't have room.

When dinner was ready, the bishop went into another room and carried out an elderly woman, took her over to the table, and gently sat her down at one of the places. Then he put a napkin around her neck and pushed her chair up close to the table. And then he went back to that room and came out with an elderly man in his arms. He carried the man over to the table, set him down on a chair next to the woman, and put a napkin around his neck. And then everyone else sat down.

The bishop told Brother Cowley, "These are two of the reasons we don't have room for you to stay here. These are the parents of my wife, and we are trying to get even with them now, while they are so helpless, for what they did for my wife when she was just a baby, a helpless child." Then, before the bishop and his wife ate, they fed the lovely parents, who were unable to feed themselves.

I ask again: How much attention is fair? How much attention is proper? How much attention is right? Where are we placing our attention? Thank the Lord for people who have room for those who need it most, regardless of title or rank or position.

Some years ago police in the District of Columbia auctioned off about one hundred unclaimed bicycles. "One dollar," said an eleven-year-old boy as the bidding opened on the first bike. The bidding, however, went much higher. "One dollar," the boy repeated hopefully each time another bike came up. And he was always the low bidder.

The auctioneer, who had been auctioning stolen or lost bikes for forty-five years, noticed that the boy's hopes seemed to soar highest whenever a racer bicycle was put up for auction. There was one racer bike left, and the bidding mounted to eight dollars. (You can tell this was a few years ago.) "Sold," said the auctioneer, "to that boy over there for nine dollars." He took eight dollars from his own pocket and asked the boy for his dollar. The youngster turned it over—in pennies, nickels, dimes, and quarters—and took his bike and started to leave. But he went only a few feet. Carefully parking his new, priceless possession, he went back, threw his arms around the auctioneer's neck, and cried.

May I ask again: How much attention is fair? Do you give this kind of attention?

In the Savior's life and teachings, how much attention is fair? Do you recall the story of the adulteress, who some said should be stoned? The Prince of Peace, the Master, took time for someone caught in the very act of a grievous sin. How much time is fair? One sinner? One Savior? Did he seek the popular? Did he seek the wealthy and the most talented? I think not. I think he gave attention where attention was deserved.

Now, going back to the purpose of it all, let me ask: How do we look upon ourselves? How much attention is fair? In First Samuel we read: "It came to pass . . . that [Samuel] looked on Eliab, and said, Surely the Lord's anointed is before him [the Lord]. But the Lord said unto Samuel, Look not on his countenance, or on the height of his stature; because I have refused him: for the Lord seeth not as man seeth; for man looketh on the outward appearance, but the Lord looketh on the heart." (1 Samuel 16:6–7.)

Let us not look at the outward appearance but rather let us look at the soul — even our own. When we think of human souls, others' and our own, all the attention in the world is not only fair but pleasing to God.

CHAPTER 9

"He Loveth That Which Is Right"

On the fourth floor of the Salt Lake Temple is the beautiful room where the First Presidency and the Council of
the Twelve meet weekly to discuss Church affairs as they
pertain to worldwide structuring and management. The
room, which is approximately fifty feet wide, fifty feet long,
and has a ceiling height of twelve feet, is decorated in pastel
colors. In the front of this room are three chairs for the
First Presidency. In a semicircle across the room from them
are twelve chairs, where members of the Twelve sit. In this
setting of privacy and warmth, the various divisions, de-
partments, councils, programs, and needs of the Church
are studied and reviewed, needs are discussed, decisions are
made, and calls to service are determined.

On the front wall of this room are three paintings by
Harry Anderson. One painting, titled "Christ Calling Peter
and Andrew," is of the Savior in white robes walking along
a seashore. He is beckoning to Peter and Andrew, who are
on a fishing boat with other fishermen, to follow him and
"be fishers of men."

Another painting, titled "The Crucifixion," is a rendering of the Savior hanging on a cross at Calvary, flanked

by two thieves who are also hanging on crosses. Numerous observers, including Mary, the mother of Christ, Mary Magdalene, other mourners, and Roman soldiers are gathered around the crosses. Thunderclouds are gathering in the sky.

The third painting, titled "The Resurrection," depicts Mary in the garden by the open tomb, looking up at the resurrected Christ before his ascension.

Around the room are paintings of the presidents of the Church. The only other picture in the room is of Joseph Smith's brother Hyrum. It is appropriate that the portrait of this great man be on display with the paintings of the Savior and the prophets of this dispensation. Hyrum was not only a brother and advocate of Joseph Smith, but to all of us who meet in the temple regularly he was also the personification of integrity. The Lord called him "blessed" and said that he loved him "because of the integrity of his heart, and because he loveth that which is right before me." (D&C 124:15.)

In Section 11 of the Doctrine and Covenants are some instructions, guidelines, and promises given by the Lord for Hyrum Smith:

"Now, as you have asked, behold, I say unto you, keep my commandments, and seek to bring forth and establish the cause of Zion. Seek not for riches but for wisdom; and behold, the mysteries of God shall be unfolded unto you, and then shall you be made rich. Behold he that hath eternal life is rich.

"Verily, verily, I say unto you, even as you desire of me so it shall be done unto you; and if you desire, you shall be the means of doing much good in this generation. Say nothing but repentance unto this generation. Keep my commandments, and assist to bring forth my work, according to my commandments, and you shall be blessed. Behold, thou hast a gift, or thou shalt have a gift if thou wilt desire of me in faith, with an honest heart, believing in the power of Jesus Christ, or in my power which speaketh unto thee." (D&C 11:6–10.)

In section 138, verse 33, Hyrum is listed as one of the mighty ones in the spirit world who were taught "faith in God, repentance from sin, vicarious baptism for the remission of sins, the gift of the Holy Ghost by the laying on of hands." And verse 55 reveals that Hyrum was "among the noble and great ones who were chosen in the beginning to be rulers in the Church of God."

The role of Hyrum Smith in the restoration of the gospel subsequent to the organization of the Church was second only to that of his brother Joseph. History points out that the Prophet did nothing of importance without first counseling with Hyrum. Whenever he was in trouble or danger or had heavy burdens, he sought out his older brother for help and advice. Hyrum was always wise and consistent.

Joseph's faith and trust in Hyrum were displayed in the beginning of the Nauvoo period. Hyrum acted as president of the Church while Joseph went to Washington, D.C., to obtain redress for the Church's losses in Missouri. Hyrum was a peacemaker, a man of integrity, an honest individual. It was said of him that he would never knowingly offend anyone. Nevertheless, he was relentless in hating wrong.

On one occasion Joseph said that if Hyrum could not make peace between two men who were in disagreement, the angels themselves might not hope to accomplish the task. About June 20, 1844, only a few days before the martyrdom, "Joseph urged Hyrum to take his family to Cincinnati for safety. Hyrum answered simply, 'Joseph, I cannot leave you.' " (Pearson H. Corbett, *Hyrum Smith, Patriarch*, Salt Lake City: Deseret Book, 1963, p. x.)

It is not uncommon that when a younger brother is highly honored, the elder brother manifests a spirit of jealousy, envy, and resentment, sometimes resulting in discontent and open opposition. But not so with Hyrum. He accepted the great vision and mission of his brother Joseph in the most sacred and loyal spirit of humility. On one occasion when William Smith, the Prophet's younger brother, took occasion to abuse Joseph with words of violence, Hyrum came to Joseph's defense. This elicited the following expression of appreciation from Joseph: "I could pray in my heart that all my brethren were like unto my beloved brother Hyrum, who possesses the mildness of a lamb, and the integrity of a Job, and in short, the meekness and humility of Christ; and I love him with that love that is stronger than death, for I never had occasion to rebuke him, nor he me, which he declared when he left me today." (*History of the Church* 2:338.)

Hyrum was always honest in his dealings with his fellowmen. He was trusted and believed. It is reported he could shoe an ox, plow, sell books, trade potatoes, preach a funeral sermon, try a case, administer the sick, ordain, rebuke the wicked, give counsel, aid the poor, perform ordinances, and preach the gospel with equal effectiveness.

On one occasion Joseph Smith, Sr., laid his hands upon Hyrum's head and blessed him thus: "My son, Hyrum, I seal upon your head your patriarchal blessing, which I placed upon your head before, for that shall be verified. In addition to this, I now give you my dying blessing. You shall have a season of peace, so that you shall have sufficient rest to accomplish the work which God has given you to do. You shall be as firm as the pillars of heaven unto the end of your days. I now seal upon your head the patriarchal power and you shall bless this people. This is my dying blessing upon your head, in the name of Jesus. Amen." (*Hyrum Smith, Patriarch,* p. 240.)

When Oliver Cowdery lost his standing in the Church, the Lord transferred to Hyrum Smith all the power and authority that had been given to Oliver, and Hyrum became the associate president of the Church, holding these keys jointly with his brother Joseph and standing with him at the head of the great and last dispensation.

After sharing many persecutions and life-threatening experiences together, the Prophet wrote: "There was Brother Hyrum who next took me by the hand—a natural brother. Thought I to myself, Brother Hyrum, what a faithful heart you have got! Oh may the Eternal Jehovah crown eternal blessings upon your head, as a reward for the care you have had for my soul! O how many are the sorrows we have shared together; and again we find ourselves shackled with the unrelenting hand of oppression. Hyrum, thy name shall be written in the book of the law of the Lord, for those who come after thee to look upon, that they may pattern after thy works." (*History of the Church* 5:107–8.)

President David O. McKay frequently said: "It is better to be trusted than to be loved." A good friend of mine learned the importance of this and the significance of being a person of integrity at a relatively young age.

In one of her high school classes, students were required

to attend a lab period early in the morning, before school officially began. In order to get credit for the lab, students would sign their names in a roll book on the teacher's desk at the beginning of the class period. One morning while my friend was standing in line waiting to sign the book, Roxanne, a popular girl who was standing in the doorway, motioned to her. She went over to Roxanne, who asked her if she would sign her name for her so that she could get credit for attending the class even though she wouldn't actually be there. Without hesitation, my friend said, "Sure, I'll do that for you." She didn't really know Roxanne very well, only that she was someone who was very popular.

My friend went back to the teacher's desk and signed her name and then Roxanne's name below her own. The teacher was obviously smarter than my friend. In the middle of the lab session she announced that there was a discrepancy in the number of students who had signed the roll and the number who were in class. Because the handwriting was the same, she knew that my friend had signed Roxanne's name. She called out her name and asked that she go to the back of the room while the rest of the class continued their lab assignments.

The teacher then proceeded to impress upon my friend an important lesson, one that she was never to forget. She can't remember most of what the teacher said to her, but she does remember that she was embarrassed. And she also remembers one question the teacher asked: "Why were you willing to sacrifice your integrity for the sake of that girl?" You see, my friend was a very good student, one who was trusted and respected, and she had let her teacher down. She was willing to sacrifice something that was most precious

72

to her because of peer pressure, because of the fear that someone wouldn't like her if she didn't do a favor for her. My friend learned that it is more important to be trusted than to be loved, that a person's integrity is of supreme importance.

Never in the history of mankind or of the Church has there been a greater need for honesty in personal lives. Honesty with neighbors. Integrity in discussions. Full trust and respect from those who are about us. Certainly we have reason to be disappointed and concerned when we see business and professional associates adopting as the best policy not honesty, but, What can I get away with without being caught? What is expedient? What will be the most profitable, the most rewarding for me, without regard for others?

Integrity must be the foundation of moral life. In our daily associations we must teach and practice the principle that honesty must be 100 percent and not treated as a means of convenience or escape. We must fight corruption and graft and help return people to the basics of integrity, honesty, and fair play. Achievement and talent without character are hollow.

Dr. Madison Sarratt, who taught mathematics at Vanderbilt University for many years, would tell his class before a test something like this: "Today I am giving two examinations—one in trigonometry and the other in honesty. I hope you will pass them both. If you must fail one, fail trigonometry. There are many people in the world who can't pass trig, but there is no one who can't pass the examination of honesty."

The Lord said to Hyrum Smith: "Behold, I speak unto you, Hyrum, a few words; for thou also art under no condemnation, and thy heart is opened, and thy tongue loosed; and thy calling is to exhortation, and to strengthen the church continually. Wherefore thy duty is unto the church forever, and this because of thy family." (D&C 23:3.)

When we think about honesty and integrity, it is well for us to ask: How will I feel tomorrow about my conduct today? Will character and integrity be the foundation of all my performances?

Jesus said, "I am the bread of life." (John 6:15.) "I am the light of the world." (John 8:12.) "I am the door." (John 10:9.) "I am the good shepherd." (John 10:11.) "I am the way, the truth, and the life." (John 14:6.) Hyrum Smith made these goals and characteristics part of his life on a continuing, steadfast basis.

As I look at that picture of Hyrum Smith in the Salt Lake Temple, I am impressed with his life, his attitude, and the love that the Lord has for him. The Lord will always have a special love for those who embrace the right. May God help us to realize that in Hyrum Smith is a man who is a worthy example today as he was in the early history of the Church — firm, steadfast, and true not only to his brother, the Prophet Joseph, but also to the Savior, Jesus Christ, and his Eternal Father. May we, when we hear of him or see his picture, recommit ourselves to the principles that he lived for and died for, and may our chosen paths lead us to do what is right. The consequences of doing what is right will bring personal victory and the love and continuing trust of the Lord.

CHAPTER 10

Learning to School Our Feelings

School thy feelings, O my brother;
Train thy warm, impulsive soul
Do not its emotions smother,
But let wisdom's voice control.
School thy feelings; there is power
In the cool, collected mind.
Passion shatters reason's tower,
Makes the clearest vision blind.

School thy feelings; condemnation
Never pass on friend or foe,
Though the tide of accusation
Like a flood of truth may flow.
Hear defense before deciding,
And a ray of light may gleam,
Showing thee what filth is hiding
Underneath the shallow stream.

Hearts so sensitively molded
Strongly fortified should be,
Trained to firmness and enfolded
In a calm tranquility.
Wound not willfully another;
Conquer haste with reason's might;
School thy feelings, sister, brother;
Train them in the path of right.
(*Hymns*, no. 336)

These words were written by Charles W. Penrose, a missionary who had been hurt by vicious gossip, slander, and lies. While being hurt to the core of his soul, he wrote these words for himself. They were not intended to be put to music and sung, but for his own discipline and guidance, he said.

The process of schooling our feelings under all circumstances is one of the greatest challenges of life. As we learn to accomplish it, it becomes a tremendous power. When we are hurt, misunderstood, ignored, belittled, wrongfully accused, disappointed, unfairly treated, and so on, we must master the situation by schooling our feelings. We must learn to control ourselves no matter how right we may be or how cruel the lies or accusations. We cannot live by the spirit, we cannot teach by the spirit, without letting wisdom control. People who are successful are those who dare to sail on when they find themselves in the icy waters of criticism and opposition.

When Joseph Smith went to Carthage to deliver himself up to the pretended requirements of the law, he said: "I am going like a lamb to the slaughter; but I am calm as a summer's morning; I have a conscience void of offense towards God, and towards all men. I shall die innocent, and it shall yet be said of me—he was murdered in cold blood." (D&C 135:4.) And when Jesus was on the cross, he prayed, "Father, forgive them; for they know not what they do." (Luke 23:34.) These are two great examples of schooling one's feelings when it would have been easier to yield, curse God, or give up.

Charles W. Penrose, born in 1832, was converted to the Church in England at the age of eighteen. Soon after, he was called to serve as a missionary. After he had served faithfully and well for two or three years without the advantage of purse or scrip, home, or permanent local leadership, he asked if he could be released and go to Zion. He was asked to continue on his mission for one more year. At later times he made additional requests, and he was always told the same: "We need you one more year." This went on until he had served ten years.

Many years after he immigrated to Utah, Elder Penrose stated: " 'School Thy Feelings' was written under peculiar circumstances just before I left England, after having traveled over ten years in the ministry. A sort of quiet slander had been circulated concerning me in Birmingham, by an Elder from Zion, and it had cut me to the quick." (*Improvement Era*, October 1924, p. 1110.)

"When I went to Birmingham . . . I had taken there a good deal of furniture and stuff belonging to my family that did not belong to the conference. It was intimated by one of the Elders from Zion that I was endeavoring [when reclaiming the furniture prior to moving] to lay claim to the property that belonged to the Birmingham Conference, and it touched me to the quick. I had labored then over ten years in the ministry, most of the time as traveling elder, literally without purse or scrip. I started that way and had continued, suffering a great many hardships and difficulties and trials that I need not refer to now, and this touched me right to the heart. I did not know how to bear it. Weltering under these feelings I sat down and wrote that little poem, right from my soul, and intended it for myself." (George D. Pyper, *Stories of Latter-day Hymns*, Salt Lake City: Deseret News Press, 1939, pp. 158–59.)

He explained: "There was not a word of truth in the story. An accusation was made, but there was no bottom to it, and it ruffled me. I did not care how much I might be scandalized by enemies of the Church; I had become accustomed to that. I used to say that my hide had got as tough as a hippopotamus; I did not care what an enemy said about me.

"But when an elder in the Church did that it cut me to the heart, and I felt like retaliating. But I sat down and wrote that little poem, 'School thy feelings, O my brother; Train thy warm, impulsive soul,' and so on. And that was for me. I did not intend it for anybody else, but it was giving a little counsel to myself." (J. Spencer Cornwall, *Stories of Our Mormon Hymns,* Salt Lake City: Deseret Book, 1963, p. 296.)

In an article in the *Improvement Era,* Elder Orson F. Whitney of the Council of the Twelve gives us further insight into this unusual story: "Here was one who knew himself to be 'falsely, basely slandered,' pleading, not with his accuser, but with himself, against the passing of condemnation 'on friend or foe.' . . . Except for the infamy of his act, I could almost thank 'the accuser of the brethren' for that 'quiet slander,' which wounded the poet's sensitive soul and gave as the indirect and unintended result this beautiful hymn, which has cheered and comforted for over [the] years the hearts of [hundreds] of thousands. Moreover, I will venture to assert that the would-be destroyer of his brother's fair fame did not profit by what he had done, while the one whom he wronged was benefited by the painful experience. Thenceforth he could sympathize, as never before, with those similarly placed." (*Improvement Era,* October 1924, p. 1110.)

Charles W. Penrose went on loving and serving God and rose step by step to positions of honor and influence. He later became an assistant Church historian, an editor of the *Deseret News,* a writer of missionary tracts, a member of the Quorum of the Twelve (1904), and a counselor in the First Presidency to President Joseph F. Smith and President Heber J. Grant.

Let me share with you a few experiences of "schooling thy feelings" that are important in my life.

In England we had a missionary who received a "Dear John" letter. These letters generally indicate that any deep affection or love a young woman has exhibited before the missionary went away has been terminated because she has made plans in other directions for marriage or at least is going steady with someone else and wants the missionary to know of the new relationship. When this particular missionary received such a letter, he was so upset and frustrated that he left his apartment, walked down the street, and hit the first policeman he saw. This not only caused embarrassment for the Church when it was reported in the newspaper, but also the missionary was jailed, and it took much time and effort to have him released at a later date.

Once a companion and I were speaking at a street meeting in Hyde Park in London. My companion had a number of titles as a boxing champion. While he was speaking, a man in the crowd became particularly distracting and rude, making fun of the Prophet Joseph Smith. This husky elder motioned me over to the stand and said, "You come up here and speak, and I'll take care of him." I'm grateful I had the feeling and the wisdom at that time to say to him, "You keep preaching and never mind him. We're not here to fight or quarrel with anyone."

79

Another experience in London was memorable. An apostle of the Church was visiting in the mission and asked me if I would accompany him and speak with him at Hyde Park. I spoke first, and people passing by seemed to have little interest. Then he took the soapbox pulpit and spoke, with the same kind of results. On the way back to the mission home, he indicated a grave concern that the people seemed to have no interest in religion, and The Church of Jesus Christ of Latter-day Saints in particular.

We returned to the mission headquarters by way of London's underground train system, and as we were walking from one level to another to change trains, we noticed sitting in a dark corner three little boys who were smoking cigarettes. My friend and companion, the apostle, walked over to the three boys and sternly said, "Don't smoke, don't smoke, don't smoke."

One of the three boys stood up, looked him in the face, poked his finger in his direction, and said, "Go to hell, go to hell, go to hell." I wondered what my companion's response would be. He took me by the arm and, as we walked away, made this excellent point which I have never forgotten: "Elder Ashton, that is no way to talk to boys, and I hope you won't do that when you counsel them."

I have made a point ever since to not use that approach but rather, by example and love, to try to guide people through a positive approach rather than a negative one.

On another occasion I had an opportunity to work with a very troubled elder. Every courtesy, love, and gesture of extreme patience had been used in his behalf, and he still failed to comply with the rules. He had failed in all of his assignments and relationships with his companions and had been summoned to the mission office to be given one more chance before being released.

In my presence, the mission president sat him down in the mission office and said, "This is your last chance. Elder Ashton will be your companion for the next few days, and if you fail to live up to all the rules and standards, you'll go home dishonorably." I was not pleased with this announcement, because it placed on me a heavy responsibility regarding the elder's future.

The next morning when I asked him to get up so we could prepare for our day's assignments, he said, "I can't get up. I'm sick." I left him in bed and went to meet with our morning study group. When I returned he was gone. He was gone all day, and I spent a good part of the day unsuccessfully looking for him. When he came back that night, he retired without comment or apology.

The next morning when he again refused to get up, I pulled his blankets back and said, "Get up right now." I took him by the arm to help him, letting him know that I meant business and that I had had enough excuses and worry without experiencing more. Suddenly he jumped up on the bed, doubled up his fist, and hit me in the mouth. Two of my teeth went through my lip, resulting in profuse bleeding.

When he realized what he had done and what the president had said about this being his last chance, he looked at me and said, "Now what do I do?" I replied, "Go to our study meeting this morning. The president will be here, and he can decide then what will happen to you."

I patched a little bandage on my lip and we went to our study group. It happened to be my turn to give the lesson, and the mission president, seeing me, asked, "What happened to your lip?" I said, "Oh, it's okay. I just did something stupid this morning."

With this comment, no more was said. The elder sat in amazement, clearly expecting me to tell the president what had happened. Through this experience and my capacity at that time to school my feelings rather than explode, he was impressed and changed his life. He remained on his mission and completed it with reasonable success.

I remember another time talking to one of our missionaries who came from a broken family. His mother was a member of the Church, but his father was not. When I asked him "How often do you write your nonmember father?" he said, "Never. I hate him." I encouraged him to write to his father and work at bridging the breach that had been building up and deepening with each passing month, but he refused to take the suggestion and wasted a lot of time hating his father. Had he learned to school his feelings and humbled himself, the result might have been quite different. But his stubbornness got in the way, and it affected his missionary work.

Some time ago, I was personally offended and hurt by something that an acquaintance had reported or shared that was untrue. It wasn't major, but it was offensive enough to upset me. I decided to call the person who was spreading the rumor and tell him that I didn't intend to tolerate his indiscretion. But first I talked to my sweetheart, Norma, and told her of my feelings and what I intended to do about it. Though she thought my cause was just and he was entitled to hear how I felt, she asked one favor. Instead of phoning him right now, she said, would I mind waiting and doing it in the morning? I agreed, and because of that wait, I never did make the phone call. As I look back now, I am glad it was not only delayed but never became an issue.

Finally I would like to share a more recent experience. The father of a missionary in the field died after a long illness. The missionary was so upset when he heard that his father had passed away that he told his companion he was going to return home to be with his family and thus show respect for his father.

His junior companion suggested that he not even think of going home, because that was not in accordance with missionary policy. He knew that if a loved one passed away, it was the missionary's duty to stay where he was, complete his mission, and pay respect by renewed effort, determination, and performance.

The missionary did not receive this counsel well, and so a zone leader was called in to counsel with him. He too gave many reasons why it would be best for the missionary to remain in the mission field, but this advice was rejected as well. Then the mission president counseled with the missionary, but to no avail. His bishop telephoned him, his stake president telephoned him, and his mother telephoned him. Each one asked him to remain and finish his mission. Each one pointed out that his father, whom they knew well, would have wanted it that way. But despite all of the counseling, the missionary decided he was going home, and nothing or no one could change his mind. He went home for the funeral.

I had been invited by the family to speak at the funeral, and as I went to the viewing before services in the chapel, a number of people said to me, "Please say something to him to shake him up so that he will realize the error of his ways and get on with his mission and life."

As I walked into the room, I noticed the elder standing beside his mother at the head of the casket. I pondered and prayed and wondered what I could say to help him, and when the moment finally came, I looked him in the eyes and, instead of saying "You ought to be ashamed. You know better than this. How come you have disappointed all of us?" I simply said, "Elder, where is your companion?"

He stood there with his missionary label on his lapel. Many people had talked to him, all to no avail. But when he was asked this question, there could be no confusion in his mind, no satisfactory answer. He had come home. He had left his companion. And he knew he had violated the rules. This question had an effect on him when other comments seemed to have failed. He later returned to the mission field and finished his term of labor.

May I repeat, Don't let your feelings be hurt. Some allow themselves to be offended when there is no intention to hurt, embarrass, or offend. In life as in athletics, the opponent has the advantage if we lose composure and concentration. Souls must be trained just as much as minds. Thank God for Charles W. Penrose, his life, and his message of "School Thy Feelings." God recognized him and honored him because he lived and trained himself in the path of right and schooled his feelings well. God will bless us also as we learn to school our feelings. May we each remember to be more patient and more considerate of others, and to always "conquer haste with reason's might."

CHAPTER 11

A Voice of Perfect Mildness

One of the great blessings of my life is to have had the opportunity of working closely with five presidents of the Church—David O. McKay, Joseph Fielding Smith, Harold B. Lee, Spencer W. Kimball, and Ezra Taft Benson. Among their great traits, I found each of them to be humble, soft-spoken, mild, kind, and gentle in leadership roles and relationships. Intimate experiences with each have helped me to know what I share here in firmness and conviction about mild voices.

Personal calls and associations with our prophets over the years have prompted me to appreciate the message in the Book of Mormon concerning the Lamanite and Nephite dissenters who were in prison and who heard a voice "as if it were above the cloud of darkness": "And it came to pass [that] they heard this voice, and beheld that it was not a voice of thunder, neither was it a voice of great tumultuous noise, but behold, it was *a still voice of perfect mildness,* as if it had been a whisper, and it did pierce even to the very soul." (Helaman 5:29–30; italics added.)

We need to listen to our leaders who administer with still voices and humble words. Too often today people are impressed with the loud, the noisy, and the dramatic. Too often we ignore the quiet promptings of our leaders and those who guide with soft words.

I had the special honor and privilege of being the last General Authority President David O. McKay called before his death. I recall with fear and trembling the impressions I had as I visited with him in his Hotel Utah apartment. I found him to be advanced in years and very weak physically. His body was frail, his voice was soft, and words did not come easily. I sat in uncomfortable silence, waiting for him to advise me as to the purpose of the appointment and visit. Finally he said, in a still voice of perfect mildness, "I want you to help me." That was my invitation, my call to be a General Authority. That was one of my unforgettable quiet experiences with President David O. McKay.

After leaving his office, I felt that I had a better understanding about the Savior's calling of his associates. Whether it was on the shores of Galilee or in the shops or paths of life, I am certain that his invitation could have been nothing more than "I want you to help me in proclaiming the gospel and being special witnesses to and for me." This experience brought me close to President McKay, a man I had loved, admired, and respected over the years. Before this intimate association, I always believed that being called to serve as a General Authority would be a complex procedure.

Often as I prepare for conference talks, I find myself turning to the life and writings of President David O. McKay. He had a beautiful, intelligent capacity not only to say things in a meaningful way, but to do so with warmth and spirit. He was a gentle man of high education and lofty principles. He had a way of making me want to do better with each performance and assignment. I will always be grateful to him because he quietly called me, expected me, and wanted me to perform special service with him. I left my occupation and former business activities and responsibilities to help him as a prophet. I tremble today as I remember how he called me with a whisper that pierced my soul.

All of my life I had a tremendous respect and high regard for President Joseph Fielding Smith as a scholar of the scriptures, a historian, and a writer. He was precise and firm in his style of living. What a blessing it was for me, when I came into the Council of the Twelve after two years as an Assistant to the Twelve, to feel of the sweet love and respect he had not only for God but also for his associates. He was kind but at the same time visionary and rigidly committed. He always took time to express appreciation, not only to his Heavenly Father but also to his associates. I will never forget his kind expressions of encouragement to me. He loved the Lord and the Lord loved him. He too called me with a soft and mild voice of deep strength.

When I was ordained an apostle and set apart as a member of the Council of the Twelve, under the hands of President Smith, the charges I received were indelibly impressed upon my mind, particularly to be a special witness by example, word, and gentleness. I was also told to listen to the still voice of the Spirit that would now come in more frequent and powerful sequence in my life.

Joseph Fielding Smith received his patriarchal blessing from Patriarch Joseph D. Smith in 1913. In this sweet and gentle blessing, he was promised that he would never be confounded as he defended the divinity of the Prophet Joseph Smith's mission. The patriarch said, "You have been blessed with ability to comprehend, to analyze, and defend the principles of truth above many of your fellows, and the time will come when the accumulative evidence that you have gathered will stand as a wall of defense against those who are seeking and will seek to destroy the evidence of the divinity of the mission of the Prophet Joseph; and in this defense you will never be confounded."

Often, over the years of our association, I felt the intense strength of President Smith as he served in mildness and with a soft voice.

On many occasions I heard President Harold B. Lee share his powerful testimony in perfect mildness. I share this example: "With all my soul and conviction, and knowing the seriousness and import of that testimony, I tell you that I know that he lives. I am conscious of his presence much of the time when I have needed him most; I have known it out of the whisperings of the night, the impressions of the daytime when there were things for which I was responsible and on which I could receive guidance. So I testify to you and tell you that he is closer to the leaders of this Church than you have any idea. Listen to the leaders of this Church and follow their footsteps in righteousness, if you would learn not only by study but also by faith, which testimony I bear most humbly and sincerely in the name of the Lord Jesus Christ. Amen." (Conference Report, April 1968, pp. 131–32.)

President Lee was one of the most spiritual leaders I have ever known. He seemed to continually possess the whisperings of the Spirit. He encouraged me to lead in mildness and quiet patience.

President Lee shared the following experience he had while serving as president of the Pioneer Stake in Salt Lake City. He felt there was a lesson in it for all. He titled it "Tune in the Lord." I love his soft-spoken yet powerful counsel in this story:

> We had a very grievous case that had to come before the high council and the stake presidency that resulted in the excommunication of a man who had harmed a lovely young girl. After a nearly all-night session that resulted in that action, I went to my office rather weary the next morning and was confronted by a brother of this man whom we had had on trial the night before. This man said, "I want to tell you that my brother wasn't guilty of what you charged him with."
>
> "How do you know he wasn't guilty?" I asked.
>
> "Because I prayed, and the Lord told me he was innocent," the man answered.
>
> I asked him to come into the office and we sat down, and I asked, "Would you mind if I ask you a few personal questions?"
>
> He said, "Certainly not."
>
> "How old are you?"
>
> "Forty-seven."
>
> "What priesthood do you hold?"
>
> He said he thought he was a teacher.
>
> "Do you keep the Word of Wisdom?"
>
> "Well, no." He used tobacco, which was obvious.
>
> "Do you pay your tithing?"
>
> He said, "No"—and he didn't intend to as long as that blankety-blank-blank man was bishop of [his ward].
>
> I said, "Do you attend your priesthood meetings?"
>
> He replied, "No, sir!" and he didn't intend to as long as that man was bishop.
>
> "You don't attend your sacrament meetings either?"
>
> "No, sir."
>
> "Do you have your family prayers?" and he said no.
>
> "Do you study the scriptures?" He said well, his eyes were bad, and he couldn't read very much.
>
> I then said to him: "In my home I have a beautiful instrument called a radio. When everything is in good working order we can dial it to a certain station and pick up the voice of a

speaker or a singer all the way across the continent. . . . But after we have used it for a long time, the little delicate instruments or electrical devices on the inside called radio tubes begin to wear out. . . . The radio may sit there looking quite like it did before, but because of what has happened on the inside, we can hear nothing.

"Now," I said, "you and I have within our souls something like what might be said to be a counterpart of those radio tubes. We might have what we call a 'go-to-sacrament-meeting' tube, a 'keep-the-Word-of-Wisdom' tube, a 'pay-your-tithing' tube, a 'have-your-family-prayers' tube, a 'read-the-scriptures' tube, and, as one of the most important—one that might be said to be the master tube of our whole soul—we have what we might call the 'keep-yourselves-morally-clean' tube. If one of these becomes worn out by disuse or inactivity—we fail to keep the commandments of God—it has the same effect upon our spiritual selves that a wornout tube has in a radio.

"Now then," I said, "fifteen of the best-living men in the Pioneer Stake prayed last night. They heard the evidence and every man was united in saying that your brother was guilty. Now you, who do none of these things, you say you prayed, and you got an opposite answer. How would you explain that?"

Then this man gave an answer that I think was a classic. He said, "Well, President Lee, I think I must have gotten my answer from the wrong source." And, you know, that's just as great a truth as we can have. We get our answers from the source of the power we list to obey. If we're following the ways of the devil, we'll get answers from the devil. If we're keeping the commandments of God, we'll get our answers from God. (*Stand Ye in Holy Places*, Salt Lake City: Deseret Book, 1974, pp. 135-38.)

Though President Lee served as our prophet for only eighteen months, the shortest period of any prophet in our dispensation, he had tremendous impact upon my life. By example he encouraged me to be quietly fearless in approaching and solving problems and in individual behavior. At the same time he pointed the way for me to show a warmth and tenderness in working with all mankind, regardless of where they had been or what they had done. Daily contact with him taught me that he could be firm and totally objective, while at the same time he had one of the most tender hearts I have ever witnessed.

An unforgettable and frightening experience I once had with President Lee occurred when he invited me to his home to participate in giving a blessing to a mutual friend who was very ill. As we gathered with a few family members, President Lee asked me if I would anoint the brother's head with consecrated oil. This I did humbly. I had never before had the opportunity of having a prophet of God seal an anointing that I would pronounce.

I recall with vividness even today President Lee's sealing of this ordinance. It seemed to me he was struggling for words, direction, and guidance to give encouragement to this good brother. I had the feeling that he wanted to promise our friend complete recovery and health from a serious malady, but the words didn't come as he pronounced the sealing. It was evident as the seconds passed that he was not only troubled but also groping for direction that would be positive and rewarding both to the recipient and to others in the room who were gravely concerned about the man's health. President Lee did not promise health, strength, and recovery to this individual. He gave words of encouragement and touched on the basics of the total gospel plan, but the promise of healing was not forthcoming.

Immediately following this experience, President Lee took me aside in another room and said softly and in perfect mildness, "Marv, he's not going to get better, is he?" I responded, "No. I could tell you wanted to promise this type of blessing, but it was apparently not to be." I recall his comment as we walked away from the hearing of family members: "The Lord has other plans, and he determines not only what we promise but also what will happen."

President Spencer W. Kimball was a prophet of love. He loved God, our Savior Jesus Christ, and all mankind. He was a constant example of warmth and Christlike love. His voice was one of perfect mildness, sometimes even less than a whisper. He was always gentle, firm, and fearless.

Here are some gentle statements that President Kimball made just after he became president of the Church. All of these seem to be filled with deep love and self-control. His voice was never one of thunder, but rather one of perfect mildness and love.

On the Church's policy on excommunication: "I think that it will remain in large measure as it has been. President Lee had felt very deeply that there must be some discipline in order to keep the Church clean and free from the sins of the world."

On blacks and the priesthood: "I am not sure that there will be a change, although there could be. We are under the dictates of our Heavenly Father, and this is not my policy or the Church's policy. It is the policy of the Lord who has established it, and I know of no change, although we are subject to revelations of the Lord in case he should ever wish to make a change."

On the state of affairs in America: "We believe that our people should sustain all the righteous activities and actions of their leaders. We do not feel that there is going to be any total disruption. We have hopes that all may straighten out well and that America might go forward. We are teaching our people to be true and loyal to their respective governments."

92

On our message to the members of the Church: "Our message is what it has always been, and our hope is that our people will live the commandments of the Lord. They have been revealed in the holy scriptures and by the living prophets through these many years." (*Ensign,* February 1974, pp. 6–7.)

President Spencer W. Kimball was one of the kindest and most courageous men I have ever met. His capacity to meet life's issues, life's disappointments, and life's successes with a proper balance and attitude is something I shall never forget. How sweet, how humble and sincere was his leadership style. His whispering voice pierced every heart that would listen.

He was courteous, friendly, and willing to be the servant of all. It was his leadership style to never demand or use the influence of his mighty calling to take the lead in what people would do or how they would respond to him. He had the kind of approach, humility, mildness, and love that would inspire all of us to sustain and support him and love him under all conditions.

A few days before he passed away, he met on the fourth floor of the temple with his counselors in the First Presidency and the members of the Twelve. He was so weak and frail that there was every good reason that he should not have been there. Before our meeting started, members of the Twelve walked by to shake his hand and greet him. There was almost no response at all because of the physical drain that had come to him over the last number of months. There was almost no capacity to communicate or respond to the present situation. His hearing was very limited, his eyesight failing, his frail body filled with aches. I shook his hand and, feeling little or no response, gave it an extra squeeze. I said, "President Kimball, I'm Marv Ashton." I will never forget his last words to me when he looked up just a little and said very softly, "Marv Ashton, I love you."

President Ezra Taft Benson is a special friend. I love him and have respect for his life and leadership. He has always conveyed to me a relationship of complete trust and confidence. This sustaining reassurance on his part has made it possible for me, in near or in distant places in the Church, to make decisions and calls that would be worthy because I knew he expected me to do just that.

I have admired his constant reminder to all, not just his associates in high levels of the Church but all members, to work with diligence in building God's kingdom and in improving our personal lives. He is a man of total obedience. I have seen him following to the letter those paths of righteousness that the Lord has given him the responsibility to point, direct, and lead. I have seen him cry unashamedly as he has talked about the wonders, content, and future of the Book of Mormon. Those of us who have been close to him have admired and respected the depth of his comment, when we were making decisions of great importance, to simply say, "Let us do what is best for the kingdom."

Besides days, weeks, and months of close association, I recall conference sessions with him — ward, stake, regional, and general conferences — where he has taken the occasion in the beginning to give encouragement and at the conclusion to offer thanks for the contributions some of us were able to make. He is a prophet who quietly builds up, delegates, and expects commitments that are unwavering.

I have always enjoyed his referring to me as one of his

brethren. I recall one telephone call I made to him while I was away on a stake assignment. A major problem was evident, and it was serious enough that I felt the need for his wise counsel and advice. After I explained the facts to him, he said in reassuring mildness and trust, "Do what needs to be done. You have my complete confidence and support."

President Benson's voice today is reduced almost to a whisper. He leads the First Presidency, the Council of the Twelve, other General Authorities, and the entire church in a spirit of pure love and perfect mildness. He leads in unwavering faith and persuasion, with a soft voice and penetrating humility. In all of my years of experience with him, I have never heard him raise his voice to a shout in moments of hurt or disappointment. I have seen him discipline and direct in mildness, patience, and pure love. How gentle yet powerful have been his words and leadership.

These five prophets I have known so well have called and encouraged in a voice and spirit of perfect mildness. I thank God for them. I pray God to help us remember that true leaders always lead with mild voices, love, and gentle persuasion. Calls and instructions from His prophets are tender and free of condemnation. With all my heart I recommend that we accept their leadership as we are invited to serve and improve our daily performances. May we always listen to the gentle promptings of the Spirit. Most often hopes and prayers are best answered by impressions of perfect mildness.

CHAPTER 12

"Stalwart and Brave We Stand"

Many years ago I witnessed a state-championship high-school track meet at Brigham Young University. A lesson I learned as I watched the mile run was most impressive. I know I shall never forget it.

About a dozen young men had qualified to represent their schools. The starting gun was fired, and these young men who had trained so long and so hard took off. Four of them, closely bunched together, took the early lead. Suddenly the runner in second place spiked the first runner's foot with his shoe. As the leader was about to make the next stride forward, he found that he was without a shoe.

Seeing this, I wondered what the leader would do because of what his competitor had unintentionally done to him. It seemed to me he had a number of choices. He could take a few extra quick sprints and catch up to the fellow who had put him out of first position, double up his fist, and hit him to get even. He could run over to the coach and say, "This is what you get. I've trained all my life for this big day, and now look what's happened!" He could run off into the stands and say to his mother, father, or girlfriend, "Isn't this horrible?" or he could have sat down on the track and cried. But he did none of these things. He just kept running.

He was halfway around the first lap, and I thought to myself, "Good for him. He'll finish this first lap of the four and retire gracefully." But after he completed the first lap, he just kept running. He completed the second lap, then the third lap — and every time he took a stride, cinders were coming up through his stocking, hurting his foot. They ran on cinder tracks in those days. But he didn't quit. He just kept running.

I thought, "What an outstanding display of courage and self-discipline! What parents! What a coach! What leaders who have affected his life enough so that in a situation like this he would not stop running!" He finished the job he had to do. He did not place first, but he was a real winner. When I walked over to him at the completion of the race and congratulated him on his courageous performance, he was composed and in complete control. He was able to carry on when it would have been much easier to quit.

Just before Elder Bruce R. McConkie passed away, with his sweetheart and eternal companion, Amelia, at his bedside, some significant words were shared. As Sister McConkie held his hand during his final earthly minutes, she asked, "Bruce, do you have a message for me?" Though weak and expiring, he responded in a firm voice his last words, "Carry on."

Here was one of God's choicest servants, who had studied, pondered, and written as extensively on the life and mission of Jesus Christ as anyone else in his time, using these two powerful words for direction and encouragement. Sister McConkie has since shared with me the great importance and strength of "carry on" as time has passed. Elder McConkie knew as a special witness the importance of the scripture that tells us, "Then said Jesus to those Jews which believed on him, If ye continue in my word, then are ye my disciples indeed; and ye shall know the truth, and the truth shall make you free." (John 8:31–32.) Salvation and exaltation are here emphasized as being based primarily upon commitment and enduring.

Enduring, or carrying on, is not just a matter of tolerating circumstances and hanging in there, but of pressing forward.

One weekend I had the opportunity of attending a stake quarterly conference in Idaho. As a group of Primary children stood before the congregation and sang "I Am a Child of God," I noticed three young Primary members on the front row singing but saying nothing vocally. They were deaf; they sang with their hands. No one heard them audibly, but we received their message. They touched my spirit deeply, and it was my privilege to tell them in front of the members of that stake that our Heavenly Father heard them. Even though vocally they had said nothing, they transmitted a memorable message. In moving silence they taught of the spirit, they taught of the mind, and they taught of the heart. They had not given up singing just because they had no voice. They had been taught to carry on.

One of our most stirring anthems is "Carry On":

> Firm as the mountains around us,
> Stalwart and brave we stand
> On the rock our fathers planted
> For us in this goodly land —
> The rock of honor and virtue,
> Of faith in the living God.

They raised his banner triumphant—
Over the desert sod.
And we hear the desert singing:
Carry on, carry on, carry on!
Hills and vales and mountains ringing:
Carry on, carry on, carry on!
Holding aloft our colors,
We march in the glorious dawn.
O youth of the noble birthright,
Carry on, carry on, carry on!

We'll build on the rock they planted
A palace to the King.
Into its shining corridors,
Our songs of praise we'll bring,
For the heritage they left us,
Not of gold or of worldly wealth,
But a blessing everlasting
Of love and joy and health.
And we hear the desert singing:
Carry on, carry on, carry on!
Hills and vales and mountains ringing:
Carry on, carry on, carry on!
Holding aloft our colors,
We march in the glorious dawn.
O youth of the noble birthright,
Carry on, carry on, carry on!
                              (*Hymns*, no. 255.)

When this beautiful anthem was first shared with the Church in 1930, to say that it was timely is an understatement. Today it should be a way of life, our top priority and clarion call for young and old. I encourage our young people and leaders worldwide to carry on. Do not give up, falter, or become weary. Do not yield to the ways of the world, which can only bring unhappiness and discouragement. I love and respect young people who stand firm when outside influences would make it easy for them to fail or fall.

I thank God continually for the young men and young

women of this generation. I firmly believe that some of the finest young people who have ever lived in the history of the Church are with us today. The great majority are pioneers on the move in righteousness and truth. Most of our youth are true to the faith despite conditions of the day and are avoiding the temptations and subtleties of misconduct that tempt them on every hand. What a joy it is to reflect upon the fact that we have more young men and young women than ever before serving in the mission field today, individuals who have great commitment and are enjoying unusual success.

As we have experienced harassment, destruction, vandalism, and even the loss of lives, the attitude of our missionaries is not one of being afraid, but of marching forward in a spirit of "carry on." Few, if any, have asked for releases or transfers as the winds of fire, destruction, and danger have blown in their paths. It is a joy to see them stand firm as the mountains around us. God will continue to help them carry on, and their work will not be thwarted but will be enhanced and fruitful.

I share with you a statement of President Benson made to a gathering of young people in southern California after he became President of the Church: "For nearly six thousand years, God has held you in reserve to make your appearance in the final days before the Second Coming. Every previous gospel dispensation has drifted into apostasy, but ours will not. . . . God has saved for the final inning some of his strongest children, who will help bear off the kingdom triumphantly. And that is where you come in, for you are the generation that must be prepared to meet your God. . . . Make no mistake about it—you are a marked generation. There has never been more expected of the faithful in such a short period of time as there is of us. . . . Each day we personally make many decisions that show where our support will go. The final outcome is certain—the forces of righteousness will finally win. What remains to be seen is where each of us personally, now and in the future, will stand in this fight—and how tall we will stand. Will we be true to our last-days, foreordained mission?"

A number of years ago Peter Snell of New Zealand was the best runner in the world in the one-mile race and the 880-yard race. I had the opportunity of meeting him in Wellington, New Zealand. Later on in the week someone said to me, "Would you like to see where Peter Snell does his training and his running?" I answered yes. I was shocked when I was taken down to the beach—not to a track, but to the beach. I asked, "Where does he run?" My friends said, "He runs out close to the water where the sand comes up over his feet. There it is difficult to pull his feet out of the sand after each stride." I had an idea why, but I said to my friends, "Why does he run there?" They answered, "When he gets on a track in competition, he feels like he's floating, because he doesn't have to pull his feet up out of the wet sand."

In my mind I could see him running on that difficult track. I learned from him. A little later my friends took me to another place where Peter Snell trained, up in the mountains. When I looked for a track again, they said, "No, he runs up the steep hills. Then, when he is on the level at track meets, it is pretty easy to run." That is why he breaks records, and that is why I remember his example.

I have always been impressed with some of the statements Winston Churchill made as he served as prime minister during England's darkest days of war. Among other things, he said the following: "It is no use saying, 'We are doing our best.' You have got to succeed in doing what is necessary."

He also said, "We have before us an ordeal of the most grievous kind. . . . You ask, What is our policy? I will say: It is to wage war, by sea, land, and air, with all our might and with all our strength that God can give us. . . . That is our policy. You ask, What is our aim? I can answer in one word: It is victory, victory at all costs, victory in spite of all terror; victory however long and hard the road may be." (First statement as Prime Minister, House of Commons, May 13, 1940.)

God wants us to be victorious. He wants us to triumph over all of our foes. Stalwart and brave we must stand. God is at the helm. There is no reason for defeat.

It should be inspiring to all of us to review and reread the message of the Lord to the Prophet Joseph Smith: "My son, peace be unto thy soul; thine adversity and thine afflictions shall be but a small moment; and then, if thou endure it well, God shall exalt thee on high; thou shalt triumph over all thy foes." (D&C 121:7–8.)

God was conveying to the noble Prophet the importance of carrying on under all circumstances and situations. We promise the youth of today, with the same conviction the Lord shared with Joseph, "Thy God shall stand by thee forever and ever." (D&C 122:4.) As we carry on today, this promise is in force and is everlasting.

CHAPTER 13

Receiving Answers to Our Prayers

I recently heard about an experience of a faithful member of the Church who had been a moderately successful contractor, a builder of homes, but who, because of the economy and some poor business practices, was forced into bankruptcy. He became somewhat embittered, complaining, "I don't know what else the Lord expects of me. I pray regularly. I pay my tithes and offerings. I attend the temple regularly. I've asked the Lord to bless me. I can't understand why he has let me down."

Prayer is a powerful possession, a great resource, comfort, strength, and channel of communication. Our Father in heaven does not forsake any of his children who come to him for help. Oftentimes, however, we do not understand what is in our own best interest and what we should pray for. Sometimes we also fail to realize when our prayers are answered.

I have always been impressed with a story President Hugh B. Brown shared with me when I was serving under his direction in the British Mission. He told about his mother's encouraging message to him as he left on his mission when he was about twenty years of age:

"Hugh, do you remember when you were a little boy and you would have a bad dream or wake up in the night frightened, you would call from your room: 'Mother, are you there?' and I would answer and try to comfort you and allay your fears? As you go out into the world, there will be times when you will be frightened, when you will feel weak and have problems. I want you to know that you can call to your Heavenly Father as you used to call to me, and say 'Father, are you there? I need your help,' and do it with the knowledge that he is there and that he will be ready to help you if you will do your part and live worthy of his blessings."

Individuals pray for different reasons, but the primary purpose of prayer is to attune ourselves to our Heavenly Father so we can receive light and truth. It is light and truth that enable us to "forsake that evil one." (D&C 93:37.) From the very beginning, the Lord commanded our first parents, Adam and Eve, "Thou shalt do all that thou doest in the name of the Son, and thou shalt repent and call upon God in the name of the Son forevermore." (Moses 5:8.)

In our dispensation, the Lord has said in many revelations, "Pray always." He said that to Joseph Smith, to Martin Harris, to Thomas B. Marsh, to the Church, and to others. (See D&C 10:5; 19:38; 31:12; 20:22.) Now note carefully the Lord's words, which apply to each of us: "What I say unto one I say unto all; pray always lest that wicked one have power in you, and remove you out of your place." (D&C 93:49.) Regrettably, some of those counseled in the revelations to pray always did not heed the counsel and were removed out of their place.

Our Heavenly Father loves each of us. We are his children. He wants us to return to him. The adversary's purpose is to deter us from a course that leads to happiness and eternal life. Knowing that, our Heavenly Father ordained prayer as the means by which we could always keep contact with him and not become strangers to him.

President Heber J. Grant once said: "The minute a man stops supplicating God for his spirit and direction, just so soon he starts out to become a stranger to him and his works. When men stop praying for God's spirit, they place confidence in their own unaided reason, and they gradually lose the spirit of God, just the same as near and dear friends, by never writing to or visiting with each other, will become strangers." (*Improvement Era*, August 1944, p. 481.)

Our Heavenly Father does not want any of us to become strangers to him!

For what do we pray? As near as I can tell, the Lord has not placed any limitations on where we should pray or what we should pray for. However, he has cautioned that we are not to pray just to gratify our selfish desires. (See James 4:3.) He said: "Do not ask for that which you ought not." (D&C 8:10.)

Here are some of the Lord's admonitions on where to pray, how often, and for what we should pray:

"And again, I command thee that thou shalt pray vocally as well as in thy heart; yea, before the world as well as in secret, in public as well as in private." (D&C 19:28.)

"Call upon his holy name, that he would have mercy on you; yea, cry unto him for mercy; for he is mighty to save. Yea, humble yourselves, and continue in prayer unto him. Cry unto him when ye are in your fields. . . . Cry

105

unto him in your houses, yea, over all your household, both morning, mid-day, and evening. Yea, cry unto him against the power of your enemies. Yea, cry unto him against the devil, who is an enemy to all righteousness. Cry unto him over the crops of your fields, that ye may prosper in them. Cry over the flocks of your fields, that they may increase. But this is not all; ye must pour out your souls in your closets, and your secret places, and in your wilderness.

"Yea, and when you do not cry unto the Lord, let your hearts be full, drawn out in prayer unto him continually for your welfare, and also for the welfare of those who are around you." (Alma 34:17–27.)

One might ask, "What if I don't feel like praying?" We may all benefit by this admonition from Nephi: "If ye would hearken unto the Spirit which teacheth a man to pray ye would know that ye must pray; for the evil spirit teacheth not a man to pray, but teacheth him that he must not pray." (2 Nephi 32:8.)

Perhaps we would do well to involve ourselves in praying more quietly and continually. Strength, power, and discipline are rewards for communicating with God on a continuing personal and private basis. Quietly we can pray for the patience to have our secret prayers answered. Sometimes we fail to recognize answered prayers because we are expecting more than quiet answers.

Nephi also counsels: "I say unto you that ye must pray always, and not faint; that ye must not perform any thing unto the Lord save in the first place ye shall pray unto the Father in the name of Christ, that he will consecrate thy performance unto thee, that thy performance may be for the welfare of thy soul." (2 Nephi 32:9.)

President Brigham Young gave this counsel on the matter of praying even when we don't feel like it: "It matters not whether you or I feel like praying, when the time comes to pray, pray. If we do not feel like it, we should pray till we do. . . . You will find that those who wait till the Spirit bids them pray, will never pray much on this earth." (*Discourses of Brigham Young,* Salt Lake City: Deseret Book, 1941, p. 44.) He also said, "If I did not feel like praying . . . I should say, 'Brigham, get down here on your knees, bow your body down before the throne of him who rules in the heavens, and stay there until you can feel to supplicate at that throne of grace erected for sinners.' " (*Discourses,* p. 270.)

Pray privately, even—and perhaps especially—when you don't feel like it.

For a prayer to be efficacious, must an individual be worthy? A qualification for efficacious prayer is the sincerity of the individual. Sinners who desire to repent can have their prayers heard more readily than hypocrites who feign worthiness or hide sin. You remember the parable of the Pharisee and the publican:

"Two men went up into the temple to pray; the one a Pharisee, and the other a publican.

"The Pharisee stood and prayed thus with himself, God, I thank thee, that I am not as other men are, extortioners, unjust, adulterers, or even as this publican. I fast twice in the week, I give tithes of all that I possess.

"And the publican, standing afar off, would not lift up so much as his eyes unto heaven, but smote upon his breast, saying, God be merciful to me a sinner.

"I tell you, this man went down to his house justified

107

rather than the other: for every one that exalteth himself shall be abased: and he that humbleth himself shall be exalted." (Luke 18:10–14.)

None of us can have our prayers consistently answered, even by a merciful Father, if we do not keep the commandments and honor our covenants.

Now what about unanswered prayers? What if God doesn't answer our prayers? During the years that I have served as a General Authority, I have listened to, or observed from the lives of individuals, various reactions to prayer. Here are several examples:

A brokenhearted mother has prayed and mourned over a wayward son. In spite of her fasting and prayers, the young man continues on his wayward course.

A returned missionary prayed and received what he thought was an answer from the Lord that a particular young woman was to be his eternal companion. However, she turned down his proposal.

A brother was faithful in the Church—paying tithing, serving in the Church, and attending the temple—but he experienced failure in his marriage. He couldn't understand why the Lord didn't get his wife to change.

A missionary complained about his companion and prayed that he would be transferred to a new companionship so he could get the Spirit. His mission president, however, felt impressed to leave the companions together.

A man couldn't understand why his wife died of a terminal disease even though she was promised in a priesthood blessing that she would live to rear her family of five small children.

These are just a few examples of individuals who have

felt that their prayers were not answered, at least not properly.

Let's look at some principles that we know to be true. These principles will give us perspective to answering the question of "unanswered" prayers.

The first principle comes from the Prophet Joseph Smith: "We are looked upon by God as though we were in eternity. God dwells in eternity, and does not view things as we do." (*Teachings of the Prophet Joseph Smith*, p. 356.) God sees things from an eternal perspective, not as we view things.

The second principle is that God has given to men and women their agency so that "they are free to choose liberty and eternal life, through the great Mediator of all men, or to choose captivity and death." (2 Nephi 2:27.) Our Heavenly Father generally will not interfere with the agency of a person's choices unless he has a greater purpose for that individual. Two examples come to mind: Saul, who became the Apostle Paul, and Alma the Younger. Both of these men were deterred from their unrighteous objective of persecuting and destroying the Church of God, and both became great missionaries for the Church. But even as the Lord intervened, they were given choices. Alma, for example, was told: "If thou wilt be destroyed of thyself, seek no more to destroy the church of God." (Alma 36:11.) Our Father honors each individual's agency. He will not compel a person to truth.

The third principle has been explained well by President Spencer W. Kimball:

"If all the sick for whom we pray were healed, if all the righteous were protected and the wicked destroyed, the whole program of the Father would be annulled and the basic principle of the gospel, free agency, would be ended. No man would have to live by faith. . . .

"Should all prayers be answered according to our selfish desires and our limited understanding, then there would be little or no suffering, sorrow, disappointment, or even death, and if these things were not, there would also be no joy, success, resurrection, nor eternal life and godhood. . . .

"Being human, we would expel from our lives physical pain and mental anguish and assure ourselves of continual ease and comfort, but if we were to close the doors upon sorrow and distress, we might be excluding our greatest friends and benefactors. Suffering can make saints of people as they learn patience, long-suffering, and self-mastery. The sufferings of our Savior were part of his education." (*Faith Precedes the Miracle*, Salt Lake City: Deseret Book, 1972, pp. 97–98.)

We are to exercise faith. We are placed on earth as a probation. It is not now, nor was it ever, the intention of a wise, omniscient Heavenly Father to solve all our problems. Life is not an uninterrupted holiday. God expects us to struggle so we may become godlike. The edict from Eden was that man should eat bread by the sweat of his brow!

The fourth principle teaches us that like a wise parent, our Heavenly Father sometimes says no to our requests. It is therefore essential that we cultivate a feeling for spiritual things that will enable us to feel or recognize the occasions when he is telling us no. We must avoid the "Laman and Lemuel syndrome" of placing ourselves "past feeling" when the Lord has spoken to us through the still small voice. (1 Nephi 17:45.) Like the Savior, we must be willing to submit to God's will, not just our own desires. Remember, our

Heavenly Father said no even to his Beloved Son's request to lift the bitter cup of pain and sorrow in Gethsemane. How eternally blessed we are because God permitted his Son to complete that suffering so we would not have to suffer if we repent.

The fifth principle is this: "Whatsoever ye ask the Father in my name it shall be given you, *that is expedient for you.*" (D&C 88:64; italics added.) And again, "Whatsoever ye shall ask the Father in my name, *which is right,* believing that ye shall receive, behold it shall be given unto you." (3 Nephi 18:20; italics added.)

How do we know when something is expedient (appropriate, good, or fitting) for us? The Lord has told us: "Ask the Father in my name, in faith believing that you shall receive, and you shall have the Holy Ghost, which manifesteth all things which are expedient unto the children of men." (D&C 18:18.)

Our Heavenly Father hears the pleadings and supplications of each of us. He wants us to call on him frequently. He wants us to have his Spirit so we may discern what is expedient for us. He delights to bless us in our eternal interest. He desires us to counsel with him in "all [our] doings." (Alma 37:37.) He wants us to appreciate our many blessings. He desires us to pray for others — our loved ones, our friends and associates, even those who despise us. He wants us to be humble.

I know God hears and answers prayers. He has answered many of my prayers. I have lived sufficiently long on this earth to see that some of the prayers of my youth, which I had concluded were not answered, were indeed answered for my best good.

111

I have total confidence and faith in the wisdom and omniscience of a living, loving, merciful Heavenly Father, to be dependent on him, yet to recognize that I must make personal effort. He is approachable. As the Prophet Joseph Smith discovered, we can ask him our innermost desires and he will not upbraid.

While in the depth of personal anguish in Liberty Jail, the Prophet Joseph Smith cried to the Lord, "O God, where art thou?" That prayer was answered with a series of revelations, which are now recorded in Sections 121, 122, and 123 of the Doctrine and Covenants. The Prophet was told his adversity would be momentary; that if he endured well, he would be exalted; and that all that he was called to pass through—the persecution, affliction, and suffering—would be for his experience and his good.

God bless us to be humble, prayerful, and submissive to the Spirit and to pray for light and truth. May we pray constantly for strength, endurance, and humility. God does answer our prayers, if we will pray, listen, wait, and work.

CHAPTER 14

Get In and Get Involved

Once a student asked me, "What do you like most about your job?" My answer: "Being involved with people, working with them, and watching them build their lives."

True happiness comes when we see others responding to our teachings and words of encouragement that result in worthy conduct and achievement. When we understand that involvement means being significantly associated, scriptural expressions like "be ye doers of the word" and "be anxiously engaged" take on broader meaning and compatibility within the better ways of life.

In a newsletter titled *Insights & Innovations for the Management of Change,* we read: "Don't look. You might see. Don't listen. You might hear. Don't think. You might learn. Don't make a decision. You might be wrong. Don't walk. You might stumble. Don't run. You might fall. Don't live. You might die." To these I might add, "Don't get involved. You might be disappointed."

Involvement in others' lives does not mean domination, management, regimentation, supervision, or compulsion. It means significant association — lifting, loving, and learning together. It means living one's own life, but not alone.

Whether it be with parents, other family members, those who are blind, deaf, poor, weary, depressed, fatherless, sick, uneducated, or oppressed, we should lose ourselves in being involved and in being able to take friends from where they are and leave them better.

In *How to Be Your Own Best Friend,* authors Mildred Newman and Bernard Berkowitz write: "People say they want to be happy; yet real happiness seems like the impossible dream. Everyone reaches for it so desperately, but for many of us it never seems to come any closer. What are we doing wrong? Why are so many people dissatisfied in so many ways? Is it the times we live in? Do we expect too much? Do we want the wrong things?" And the authors, both psychoanalysts, answer, "Well, it's not as bad as all that. There are plenty of people who are having a wonderful time with their lives; they are living to the hilt and love every minute of it. But they don't talk about it much; they are busy doing it. They don't usually write articles or go to analysts. Yet it's true; not enough people have that sense of zest in their daily lives. Too many people have just not mastered the art of being happy." (New York: Ballantine Books, 1974, pp. 19–20.) May I add, "Yes, they have not learned to become properly involved."

John, the apostle, may well have expressed the feelings of a mother, father, friend, educator, or God when he said, "I have no greater joy than to hear that my children walk in truth." (3 John 3:4.) Happiness comes to us as we see others walking in truth and involving themselves in truth.

Let me share some experiences that have brought happiness to me through mutual involvement.

A friend who is an FBI agent wrote to me from New

York and said: "I am here involved in a very, very important case. The days are long and the nights are longer because I am away from my family. I have had little bit of time to think. As I have been thinking, I am impressed to write you a letter." In the letter he didn't say "I am thankful you are a member of the Council of Twelve Apostles." Rather, he said, "I want to thank you for what you did for me when I was a deacon, teaching me to be in my quorum meeting every week. I am glad that you had ten of us with 100 percent. You told us if we would be 100 percenters, you would give each of us a jacket as a reward. I still have the jacket. Thank you for what you did for me when I was a deacon."

Just before a devotional at Brigham Young University–Hawaii campus, I had the opportunity of meeting a blind girl who was not a member of the Church. As we visited, she told me briefly how she happened to come to the university. Then she mentioned that she played the piano. I asked her, "Do you know where the piano is on the stand?" She did not know what I had in mind, but she said, "Yes, I know where it is." When I was called on to speak, I diverted just a little bit and called upon her to come to the stand to play for us. As she walked up to the stand I thought, *Ashton, you dummy. What if she falls? What if she misses a step on the way up?* She walked alone, without help, and she played a beautiful piano solo. Then she walked all the way back to her seat on her own.

About a year and half later I had a telephone call in Salt Lake City. A voice said, "Elder Ashton, I don't know whether you remember me or not, but I'm the girl you called upon to give an extemporaneous performance at the piano in Hawaii. I'm now a member of the Church, and I'm going to be married next week. My parents are still not members. Would you be good enough to go to the temple with me?" Through that involvement in music and in education, we have a special friendship.

A Christmas or two later the Ashton family had the opportunity of doing a little sacrificing and pooling some funds to buy a small organ for this young woman and her husband so she could play it in her home.

These kinds of involvement bring happiness, enlarge our families, and give us purpose in life.

Sometimes our most effective involvement is simply to listen and care. For example, some time ago I visited with another college student. When we were through, and I had done what I had felt was a reasonable job of listening (sometimes that can be the most important part of counseling), she said quietly, "Thank you, Elder Ashton, for listening to me."

Horace Mann once said, "I have never heard anything about the resolutions of the apostles, but a great deal about their acts." We too will be remembered by our worthy acts of involvement in the lives of people more than by our academic or professional achievements.

True education never stops. It is not restricted to time or place. We must continue our quest of personal perfection. Joseph Smith once wisely said, "We cannot be saved until we have risen above all our enemies, not the least of which is ignorance."

Important parts of continuing improvement are appreciation, patience, determination, drive, and commitment. May I just touch briefly on one of these virtues and strengths,

116

appreciation. A truly educated person takes the time to express appreciation. We often hear the repeated phrase, "Do a good turn daily."

In D&C 59:21, our Heavenly Father tells us, "In nothing doth man offend God, or against none is his wrath kindled, save those who confess not his hand in all things, and obey not his commandments." Let us make appreciation part of our prayers. Let us make appreciation part of our lives. What a lift it is to have someone hear us say, "Thank you for what you have done to make today possible."

Camilla Eyring Kimball, the wife of President Spencer W. Kimball, said, "Some people feel that their responsibilities stifle them. I feel that fulfilling obligations is the best way to grow—the very best way. Any woman should be alive to opportunities—alive to public interests, to her family, to growth from Church service. Life is so interesting, it just worries me that I cannot get it all done. I have no patience with women whose lives bore them." (*The Writings of Camilla Eyring Kimball*, Salt Lake City: Deseret Book, 1988, p. 138.) All of her life she involved herself in personal improvement, education, service, and commitment.

"The future belongs to those who prepare for it," said Ralph Waldo Emerson. The Lord said this in a different way: "If you will that I give unto you a place in the celestial world, you must prepare yourself by doing the things which I have commanded you and required of you." (D&C 78:7.)

Achievements are attained by involvement, not dreams. Throughout life we should be actively engaged in the process of becoming the person we want to be. We should be looking for and accepting opportunities for responsibility. Every new assignment we perform well adds to our self-confidence and

117

helps remove fears that might prevent us from going where we know we should go. As we move forward by self-motivation, our faith in our own judgment will increase.

Life is difficult. It continually presents problems and challenges. But if we choose to use our education, talents, minds, and faith to solve these problems, life becomes a rewarding, growing, and exciting process. Only those who moan about their problems instead of trying to solve them become weighed down, discouraged, and depressed. They lose the opportunity to grow mentally and spiritually.

We must be willing to work with our minds and our hands, whether it be on the farm, in the warehouse, in the factory, or in an office. We must be willing to work. President N. Eldon Tanner of the First Presidency was a man heavily involved in work. Here are some things he said on this subject:

"I have always made it a point that whenever anyone came into my office under any circumstances I would work to make it possible for them to leave better than when they came in. Work to get the facts, and then make your decisions on the facts. If you lose yourself in the work, you'll be successful all your life. It isn't the mountain that is hard to climb, it is the sand that gets in your shoes. If you want your dreams to come true, you'd better wake up."

President Tanner was a man who worked on solutions — a man who worked and was victorious in the contest of life.

Much has been said over the years about family members and work, allowances, and fees that come from families and others. May I say in passing that I am from the old school. I believe that children should earn the money they need through service, appropriate chores, and involvement. It is unfortunate for children to grow up in homes where the seeds are planted in their minds that there is a family money tree that automatically drops "green stuff" once a week or once a month.

Once we have made a commitment to something or someone, we should work toward making that situation successful, so that there is no chance for failure. Success comes to those who are workers and who enjoy the challenges to be found in working. It was Thomas A. Edison who said, "I never did a day's work in my life — it was all fun."

If we are always looking for someone else to solve our problems, we will have a hard time and a lot of disappointments. We ourselves must work on and resolve the things that are important in our lives.

In the world of work, too many want to start at the top. Only in the arena of the real world can we achieve moral, physical, and mental control. Practical experiences are the added dimension we need for success, after the discipline and theory of our chosen craft or profession have been learned. There is no way to scale to the summit without climbing or to win the prize without running the race. As William James said, "The greatest use of a life is to spend it on something that outlasts it."

And finally, we must be involved in our Father's business. Remember that profound statement of young Jesus of Nazareth: "Wist ye not that I must be about my Father's business?" (Luke 2:49.) What a meaningful statement on priorities and wisdom. As Jesus became more involved in his Father's business, he became more like him.

"Love one another, as I have loved you." That is what

119

his business is all about. Without fear, without hesitation, without being ashamed, we should love one another. It is the only business that is eternal and pays dividends without fail.

Proper involvement in his business will insulate us from earthly businesses that would tempt through fraud and deceit. If we are involved in his business continually, we will not perform shabbily. Walking in his paths will prevent us from tripping over ourselves.

The greatest knowledge we can ever possess is to know God and Jesus Christ. This must be an eternal pursuit and the basic foundation of all meaningful education. "O ye that embark in the service of the Lord, see that ye serve him with all your heart, might, mind, and strength." (D&C 4:2.) Joys and rewards come from being involved in his business. The Savior has taught us, "Blessed are they which do hunger and thirst after righteousness: for they shall be filled."

May God help us to involve ourselves in people's lives, involve ourselves in personal improvement, involve ourselves in work, and involve ourselves in his business, and thereby reap the rewards that come from such commitments.

CHAPTER 15

A Voice of Gladness

Less than four months after The Church of Jesus Christ of Latter-day Saints was organized, the leaders were subjected to intense persecution. Partial seclusion had become necessary. During this trying period, the following was revealed to Joseph Smith:

"Behold, thou wast called and chosen to write the Book of Mormon, and to my ministry; and I have lifted thee up out of thine afflictions, and have counseled thee, that thou hast been delivered from all thine enemies, and thou hast been delivered from the powers of Satan and from darkness! . . .

"Be patient in afflictions, for thou shalt have many; but endure them, for, lo, I am with thee, even unto the end of thy days." (D&C 24:1, 8.)

The words "For, lo, I am with thee, even unto the end of thy days" were the Lord's voice of gladness to his beloved prophet. His message to Joseph Smith and to us is "You can do it, and I will help you."

Recently we read in local newspapers an account of the devastating effects of a fire that completely gutted a low-income-housing apartment. Many people were rushed out into the street for safety. They watched their living quarters and other earthly possessions go up in fire and smoke. One elderly gentleman who escaped the holocaust was interviewed. When he was asked "What were you able to save," he responded with, "Only the things that you see, my clothing." His next comment was touching and significant. It was, "Thank God there were no serious injuries or casualties."

What did we hear from this tragedy? A voice of gladness from someone who could have been bitter and angry with the situation, but who chose to share a mature sense of values. He was bigger than that which had happened. He saw beyond the present and gave appreciation and hope for conditions and people in the future.

Disappointments, death, losses, and failures are real and difficult to manage, but they should never cause us to have barbed tongues, lasting resentment, or negative attitudes. The gospel encourages us to develop the capacity to learn from the past and present and see the opportunities that can be ours in the days to come.

In the Doctrine and Covenants, we are given this counsel: "Now, what do we hear in the gospel which we have received? A voice of gladness! A voice of mercy from heaven; and a voice of truth out of the earth; glad tidings for the dead; a voice of gladness for the living and the dead; glad tidings of great joy. How beautiful upon the mountains are the feet of those that bring glad tidings of good things." (D&C 128:19.)

The Lord would have us mingle our voices of gladness with his to give strength, encouragement, and joy to his children.

I recall as a young boy going with my father to visit an elderly widow living in humble circumstances. We shared a couple of boxes of food with her. When we were leaving, her remarks touched my heart. She said, "Thank you, bishop, and please come back again, even if it's just to say hello."

This was probably the first time I realized that the food items were appreciated, but the words of encouragement and the personal visit were of greater value.

In the world where there are often voices of pessimism and negative feelings, the voice of gladness is welcome indeed. Some seem to live with doubt, fear of the future, and sorrow for the past. If it is our nature to criticize or demean, we can cause the voices of gladness to be silenced. We need those who bring gladness into our lives. We need those who give encouragement and reflect optimism.

Sincere yet simple words of praise can lift souls and bring gladness. Mark Twain remarked that he could live two months on one good compliment. In the words of Solomon: "A word fitly spoken is like apples of gold in pictures of silver." (Proverbs 25:11.)

Encouragement can be quick and simple, but it is a voice of gladness that is needed by everyone.

Most of the military personnel returning from active duty are willing to be examples of voices of gladness as they remind us that some things in life, like precious freedom and liberty, are more important than life itself. Many have had their lives changed permanently, but their voices of gladness overshadow the prevailing interruption and sacrifices they have made for all of us. Hope springs eternal for those who have the vision to trust in and live by God's inspired principles.

The teachings of the gospel have brought glad tidings to all the world. The subtle messages remind us of attitudes that can help us face the trials of life with less difficulty. Research has verified the fact that bitterness injures more the person who carries it than the one who caused it.

Erma Bombeck has written a book about young cancer patients. As she planned her book, she came to the conclusion that the voices that came from these young people were filled with humor and optimism that kept them "in the mainstream of life. Perhaps laughing and believing in themselves was a major part of their survival." One sixteen-year-old boy said, "Man, without a sense of humor I wouldn't have made it this far."

As the author interviewed the youths with cancer and read many letters from them, she found one word constantly surfacing: *attitude*. She wrote: "They took personal pride in the fact that they were fighting something bigger than they were and stronger than they were . . . something that might even overpower them. But they still had something their enemies couldn't take away—hope. It's a formidable weapon. . . . When all else fails, pull out the big artillery, HOPE, and hang on." (*I Want to Grow Hair, I Want to Grow Up, I Want to Go to Boise*, New York: Harper, 1989, pp. xiv, xvii, 4–6.)

Words of hope and gladness are often repeated in the scriptures to help us think and perform positively.

Isaiah says of Jesus Christ: "And when we shall see him, there is no beauty that we should desire him. . . . A man of sorrows, and acquainted with grief: and . . . despised, and we [esteem] him not." (Isaiah 53:2–3.)

But even though Jesus' suffering was beyond our com-

124

prehension, his voice of gladness reminds us: "Be of good cheer; I have overcome the world." (John 16:33.) He challenges all of us to be happy and optimistic. As the cancer patients learned and medical research has proven, "A merry heart doeth good like medicine: but a broken spirit drieth the bones." (Proverbs 17:22.)

At a regional conference in California, a well-trained multistake chorus furnished beautiful music. As I listened and watched them, I was impressed with the fact that on the front row, four individuals who were participating with the choir sang not with their voices, but with their hands. I thought to myself on that occasion how wonderful for a choir director to encourage their participation. Without the advantange of melody or audible lyrics, they were able to stand with pride and a sense of belonging to share their communication of gladness and be an inspiration to all the congregation. Deference, courtesy, and respect had made their voices of gladness strengthening and comforting.

Thank God for noble souls who can and do weather life's storms with sincere voices of gladness that overshadow the present and make the principles of the gospel of Jesus Christ real and strengthening.

"Let us therefore follow after the things which make for peace, and things wherewith one may edify another." (Romans 14:19.)

After a night of intense pain and suffering, one morning a husband stricken with a terminal illness said to his wife with great feeling, "I am so thankful today." "For what?" she asked, knowing well his difficult and trying situation. He replied, "For God giving me the privilege of one more day with you." A voice of gladness is so refreshing when an attitude of despair might be deemed appropriate.

How helpful and rewarding it would be if all of us would likewise thank God for one more day. For what? For the opportunity to take care of some unfinished business; to express appreciation; to repent; to right some wrongs; to influence for good some wayward child; to reach out to someone who is crying for help — in short, to thank God for one more day to prepare to meet him.

> Now Peter and John went up together into the temple at the hour of prayer, being the ninth hour. And a certain man lame from his mother's womb was carried, whom they laid daily at the gate of the temple which is called Beautiful, to ask alms of them that entered into the temple; who seeing Peter and John about to go into the temple asked an alms.
>
> And Peter, fastening his eyes upon him with John, said, Look on us.
>
> And he gave heed unto them, expecting to receive something of them.
>
> Then Peter said, Silver and gold have I none; but such as I have give I thee: In the name of Jesus Christ of Nazareth rise up and walk. And he took him by the right hand, and lifted him up: and immediately his feet and ankle bones received strength.
>
> And he leaping up stood, and walked, and entered with them into the temple, walking, and leaping, and praising God. And all the people saw him walking and praising God. (Acts 3:1–9.)

Now hear Peter's proclamation of glad tidings: "Ye men of Israel, why marvel ye at this? or why look ye so earnestly on us, as though by our own power or holiness we had made this man to walk?" (Acts 3:12.)

Peter through his priesthood power declared, "In the name of Jesus Christ of Nazareth rise up and walk." Then the feet of the lame man bore the glad tidings of good things to all who were in the temple to hear and see.

How impressive, encouraging, and meaningful is the

attitude of some parents who, when learning of the accidental death of their son while he was serving a full-time mission, were heard to say with perfect sweetness and understanding, "We will soon have another son available as a missionary. His time and service will also be in the hands of the Lord." Sure voices of gladness during tragedy help build women, men, and God's kingdom.

We can choose our reactions to difficulties and challenges. One way to learn how to incorporate the voice of gladness through tragedy or happiness is to learn to apply gospel principles. They teach us to never be overcome by the negative, by gloom, or by cynicism.

From guidelines given to us in the scriptures and through the words of prophets, we learn that life is a teaching experience. Self-pity and discouragement do not come from the teachings of the gospel of Jesus Christ. But life can be both bitter and sweet. It is up to us to choose whether we want to reflect the voices of gloom or those of gladness.

The voices of gladness have not always been available to the masses. In ancient days, death by fire was often the punishment for those who endeavored to read Bible manuscripts or to publish those glad works. Little by little customs were changed by valiant people. Now we have scriptures and words of prophets for us to study. With the help of the Holy Ghost, it is our opportunity to understand and live by the doctrine of salvation.

The voices of gladness from the scriptures remind us that we don't have to walk through life alone. Christ came so that we might have life and have it more abundantly. "For we know that it is by grace that we are saved, after all we can do." (2 Nephi 25:23.)

Let us remember that acts of kindness with pure motives and righteous purposes can be and are encouraged to be done in quietness, gentleness, and privacy. We can program ourselves to build, encourage, and give strength.

What a voice of gladness was shared when our Savior, Jesus Christ, following torment, ridicule, abuse, and ultimate crucifixion, in a voice of mercy, glad tidings, and truth was able to say, "Father, forgive them; for they know not what they do." (Luke 23:34.)

May I share my witness and testimony that I know God is pleased when we declare glad tidings of truth, righteousness, and his reality. My voice of gladness is that God lives. Jesus is the Christ. Let no one or any situation take this reality from you. I declare this message with a voice of gladness in the name of Jesus Christ.

CHAPTER 16

For Those Who Stand in Need

Based upon my experiences in life, I have never met a person who did not need comfort. God undoubtedly knew this full well, and that is why he has blessed us with a constant comforter, the Holy Ghost.

Comfort is more than relief from sorrow and distress. It is help, support, and assistance in all walks and times of life. It is example and courage in action as we live and associate with others. It also gives us a chance to share solace, consolation, and freedom from pain, want, or other afflictions.

Comfort is assistance in times of stress, extreme pressure, and discouragement. It encourages freedom from physical, spiritual, and mental down-days. Strong, unwavering, tested, and true associates seem to give me my greatest comfort. Their lives, standards, and commitments seem to steady the course when the unexplained and unwanted seem to surface and shackle.

May I share insights of some very special friends as I deal with comforting those who stand in need. These friends are women who are not married but who have found comfort and joy in the Church through various experiences.

1. *God is our Father.*

What joy, strength, and power we may receive if we never lose sight of this eternal truth. In our happiest or loneliest hours we need to cherish this fact.

Rebecca Coombs writes: "Heavenly Father has also given me a great deal of encouragement through priesthood blessings. Years ago, during my junior year in college, I was questioning my direction. I had just been called as a Gospel Doctrine teacher in my student ward. I prayed and fasted for a confirmation from Heavenly Father that my life was in harmony with his will. On the day I was set apart, my bishop, who had no knowledge of my personal struggle, was inspired to tell me in the blessing that I was where I was supposed to be and that I was doing what I should be doing. I was overcome with gratitude for Heavenly Father's love and care for me. I have had other such experiences since that time. I cannot adequately describe how thankful I am to know that Heavenly Father is concerned with my present happiness as well as my eternal well-being and joy." (*A Singular Life*, Carol L. Clark and Blythe D. Thatcher, eds., Salt Lake City: Deseret Book, 1987, p. 19.)

I am impressed with how Rebecca is able to relate her Heavenly Father's closeness. Her association with him is real, personal, and simple. It is comforting to have someone share the truth through personal experience that God is nearby and delights in our being happy in our assignments and life.

Cheryl Ballard shares this experience: "One bright star, Veon Riggs Shupe, a revered and long-time friend, frequently reminded me in my youth that 'God did not just throw us out into space to flop around. He gave us every ingredient for greatness that he possesses. He gave us a span of time, he gave us limitless opportunities, and he promised that we need never be alone if we would seek his companionship and remain teachable.' She counseled my friends and me to choose confidantes carefully and prayerfully and not to seek advice unless we were willing to take it. She admonished us to refrain from habitually rehearsing our tribulations, cautioning us that if we did, we would likely bleed to death emotionally and spiritually and become undesirable to our associates. Veon, a widow, was so filled with light, life, enthusiasm, fun, and good humor that we never doubted her. Her own example encouraged us to enjoy, not simply endure, the scenery of life. So it is with bright stars. Their light is contagious, and their influence immeasurable." (A *Singular Life*, p. 27.)

Sister Ballard shares a great truth when she speaks of involving God in our decisions and then having the courage to follow righteous impressions. This way God becomes a source of constant comfort.

Let us remember, in our relationships with God through prayer and daily associations, that we will receive no real comfort if we habitually rehearse our tribulations. There is strength and purpose in seeking God's help in all of our situations, but his consoling powers may fail to reach us if we are overly anxious in our complaints. Lasting comfort is not available to those who look upon life's tribulations as being unfair. Constant comfort is available to those who are anxiously engaged.

Knowing that God is a loving, caring Father will fortify us in our personal struggles. Our Heavenly Father wants us to be happy. I promise comfort to those who seek him constantly in reverential trust and dependency. He will not leave us to walk or struggle alone if we will but have childlike faith in his reality and strength.

2. *Jesus Christ is our Redeemer.*

To know Jesus, to love him, and to bear testimony of him are among the great joys of life. He not only makes life eternal possible, but he also points the way and marks the proper paths for all of us to tread. What a comfort it is to know him, the Only Begotten of the Father. He is our Savior and our advocate with the Father.

I love the message found in John 20:

> But Mary stood without at the sepulchre weeping: and as she wept, she stooped down, and looked into the sepulchre, and seeth two angels in white sitting, the one at the head, and the other at the feet, where the body of Jesus had lain.
>
> And they say unto her, Woman, why weepest thou? She saith unto them, Because they have taken away my Lord, and I know not where they have laid him. And when she had thus said, she turned herself back, and saw Jesus standing, and knew not that it was Jesus.
>
> Jesus saith unto her, Woman, why weepest thou? whom seekest thou? She, supposing him to be the gardener, saith unto him, Sir, if thou have borne him hence, tell me where thou hast laid him, and I will take him away.
>
> Jesus saith unto her, Mary. She turned herself, and saith unto him, Rabboni; which is to say, Master.
>
> Jesus saith unto her, Touch me not; for I am not yet ascended to my Father: but go to my brethren, and say unto them, I ascend unto my Father, and your Father; and to my God, and your God.
>
> Mary Magdalene came and told the disciples that she had seen the Lord, and that he had spoken these things unto her. (John 20:11–18.)

One of the reasons I love these special verses is that they powerfully share the woman's special touch. Mary not only gave comfort, but she also carried, with warmth, the sweet message that she had seen the Lord and that he had conversed with her on an intimate basis truths of eternal significance.

Shelley Swain shares some additional truths: "Lowell Bennion . . . stresses being actively involved in life rather than safely watching it go by. He encourages us to test the Lord's teachings by doing them and thus allowing the refinement to come through experience. When I read his writings, I don't want life to pass me by. I at least want to try. . . .

"The Savior and his teachings have shaped my perspective and play a continually greater role in my daily life. I love the story of the Savior telling Martha that Mary has chosen the good part by listening to his teachings rather than being too concerned about functions in the house. My role as a woman, a daughter of God, is to develop into a celestial being." (A *Singular Life,* p. 133.)

Shelley impresses me by reemphasizing the importance of all Marys and Marthas in choosing the good part. If we choose the good part, knowing that Jesus truly loves us and is our Redeemer, comfort will flow in every direction.

3. *In all things give thanks.*

"In nothing doth man offend God, or against none is his wrath kindled, save those who confess not his hand in all things, and obey not his commandments." (D&C 59:21.) This scripture has always given me grave concern. To know that we can kindle God's wrath by failing to express and show appreciation is not only frightening but also challenging. We should acknowledge his bounteous gifts continually. More and more of our time should be spent in giving thanks and reviewing our blessings. Some time should be spent every day in personally counting our blessings. Days of stress and discouragement are excellent days in which to count rather than complain.

Let me share some experiences and meaningful thoughts from Mary Ellen Edmunds:

"Several years ago, probably close to twenty years, I became aware that I spent a lot of time thinking—and worrying—about what I *didn't* have. All around me were reminders of what others had that I didn't. It wasn't so much their possessions as their situation—their home and family and children. During this time I read a little story that had a powerful effect on me. I don't remember just where I found it, but I'll never forget how it made me feel and the deep impression it left:

"Two little children were put early to bed on a winter's night, for the fire had gone out, and the cold was pouring in at the many cracks of their frail shanty. The mother strove to eke out the scantiness of the bed covering by placing clean boards over the children. A pair of bright eyes shone out from under a board, and just before it was hushed in slumber a sweet voice said, 'Mother, how nice this is. How I pity the poor people who don't have any boards to cover their children with this cold night.'

"This little story stopped me in my tracks. I thought about it over and over again, coming to the realization that I had spent far too much time in my life thinking of all I didn't have instead of all I did have. Here was a little unknown child who taught me a great lesson: she was grateful for present blessings. She was looking at everything from the perspective of what she had. And thus was born my personal theory of relativity.

My personal theory of relativity

134

"I know there will always be many people who have much, much more than I do—more time, more clothes, more talent, more hair, more pets, more toys, more children, more things—but there will also always be millions who have much, much less than I do, and in many situations much, much less than they need. I began to understand it is not what I have, but what I enjoy, that brings real happiness. My theory of relativity ties in with such hymns as 'Count Your Blessings.' I have been making a conscious effort to expect less and appreciate more. This change is making a noticeable difference in my life. It's a process, not an event, so it takes time, but I feel progress, and I am emjoying the effort. . . .

expect less appreciate more

"In the Philippines in 1973 I was serving as a health missionary, and my companion and I used to take the bus from Manila to Baguio about once a month. We began to notice one little girl who was always at the bus station in Baguio when we'd arrive. She sold peanuts and newspapers. She always had on the same ragged T-shirt, shorts, and thongs. She got so she recognized us and would run to greet us when we'd arrive. One day we took her picture. She looked at the camera curiously, and we wondered if she'd ever had her picture taken before. We took the film back to Manila and got it developed. On our next trip we brought her a picture of herself and could hardly wait to find her.

"She came running when she saw us, and I handed her the photograph, expecting her to exclaim with delight that she was happy to have it. But she took it and kept looking at it intently, finally asking, 'Who is this?'

"I couldn't believe it. Here was a little child who, in the literal sense, didn't know who she was! I said, 'It's you.'

135

" 'Me?' She looked even more closely at the picture.

" 'Yes, it's you.' Then I got an idea and pointed to the hole in her T-shirt. 'Do you see this hole? Here it is in the picture. This is your shirt, and this is you.'

"Then I could see by the look on her face that she had at last discovered it was a picture of her. She dropped the papers and peanuts and went hollering through the bus area, 'It's me! It's me! It's me!'

"Relatively speaking, I know a lot about myself and my relationship to my Father in Heaven, the Savior, the Holy Ghost, my earthly parents and brothers and sisters, and to everyone I meet. Here was a little girl who knew almost nothing about who she was and who God was. My little friend didn't know that she had kept her first estate and had the potential to return to live with God. It seemed to me that I could learn from that contrast. I could learn of gratitude for knowing who I am and for a chance to help anyone else know more about who they are, especially with regard to their relationship to their Heavenly Father and their purpose for being on this earth with the rest of us.

"These and many other experiences helped me realize how much I have and caused me to do a lot of pondering about how much I enjoy what I have and how willing I am to share. My experiences have brought me perspective and help me understand more about myself and others and about life. One thing perspective does is teach me more about why — why I was asked to do certain things at certain times in my life. I have found that for me nothing happens in isolation; it is all connected." (*A Singular Life*, pp. 140–41, 144–45.)

May I reemphasize that comfort comes from counting

136

blessings, not by complaining. Sometimes we best demonstrate appreciation by the way we share. I have seen people lift themselves to new heights by not taking the time for self-pity or personal sympathy. Pondering under all circumstances God's goodnesses to us is good therapy for the troubled heart and soul. It has been rewarding to me, when I have taken the time to properly discipline myself, to try and comfort others when I felt I was entitled to it myself. Comfort can come from many sources, but the most lasting comes from quality human beings.

4. *We must protect our self-worth.*

I like Mary Kay Stout's thoughts:

"The expectation of a cause-and-effect relationship frequently produces an assumption that we have earned, deserve, or are entitled to a specific reward such as marriage, financial security, happiness, career success, or friendships because of personal worthiness or sacrifice. Although cause-and-effect applies in many circumstances (obtaining educational degrees, or strengthening muscles), it does not necessarily apply either in building relationships with others or in receiving blessings from our Heavenly Father.

"A belief in entitlement may result in disillusionment if we feel we have not received the fulfillment and growth we have earned almost as if by contract. It is easy for us to convince ourselves that we have earned rewards according to our own timetables. 'I've been righteous, faithful, and chaste! Where are my blessings?' . . .

"Overwhelmed individuals may cope with a problem by avoiding, rationalizing, or procrastinating. It is easy to become cynical when hearing talks in church on setting goals, managing our time, and overcoming self-defeating behaviors after we have listed (or failed to list) the same January 1 goals for several years running. We frequently convince ourselves that the task will remain unapproachable and insurmountable. Many individuals who regard themselves as professionally and socially competent will admit that there are touchy issues in their personal lives that have not benefited from their formidable skills. Many of us have not developed manageable working plans for our personal equivalents to cleaning out the garage. . . .

"[Many] testify to the truthfulness of prayer, fasting, service or other gospel principles; however, their unwillingness to see the gospel as a package deal and their persistence in selecting only certain principles and programs have caused each one to succumb to individual weaknesses and appetites." (A *Singular Life*, pp. 86–87, 91, 93.)

None of us can share comfort or enjoy it if we are in a holding pattern of avoiding, rationalizing, or procrastinating. Comfort is a process, not a situation. We can take comfort and strength in ourselves as we move forward with proper self-respect and self-worth appraisals. Let us do it without delay.

I personally gain strength from Christine Timothy's comments: "Facing life one day at a time is a challenge. Continually building character is a challenge. With all those challenges, I have a choice to make: either I can go through this life being happy, knowing that my Heavenly Father knows my individual needs; or I can be miserable, by shutting out his influence in my life. I have found that with my faith, my friends, and my family I can find the way to make my journey a much happier one. I can draw from them the strength to do whatever I find is expected of me. Without them I cannot." (A *Singular Life*, p. 126.)

Comfort comes by the hour, the day, the week, the month. It is a process, not a gift given from one to another. Being miserable is generally the product of giving up and surrendering to circumstances. Certainly there can be no true comfort zone when one ceases through discouragement to build character. Comfort results from carrying on, not nursing wounds. Courage should be a constant factor in achieving joy and happiness.

There can be comfort in quiet times. Some of Mary Ellen Edmunds's thoughts on this are helpful:

"A verse in the Doctrine and Covenants impressed me very much. It's in section 88, verse 95: 'And there shall be silence in heaven for the space of half an hour.' The quality of that silence will likely be different from silence I've experienced on this earth, and I wonder what I will think about during that half hour. What will be important to me then? What is it that will bring peace of soul at that time? In that very silent, final half hour I'll think about the most important things. I'd like to do that better right now, as I look for chances to practice — during the sacrament, during prayer, during other times of pondering and meditation, during scripture study." (A *Singular Life,* p. 154.)

We must constantly dwell on building self-respect and the feeling of belonging. Doing all that we can, and leaving some things undone, can bring internal comfort. We become comfortable as we learn to adjust and fit in.

Joan Clissold, who found herself "newly single" after a divorce, shares some thoughts on these situations:

"I was not an outsider but feeling like one. . . . I began to realize that if I did not try harder to feel at home, I might develop permanent feelings of being odd or just not fitting

139

in. . . . It is important to let single people in a ward feel part of the whole without thinking that they must do everything like married people or do nothing at all. . . . Setbacks do occur, sometimes suddenly and at unexpected moments. It is then that magnified feelings of isolation and rejection return and with them the realization that I am not part of the social mainstream of the Church. These times are discouraging; fitting in does not come naturally." (A *Singular Life,* pp. 167, 168.)

Joan is extremely helpful to me in her timely observations of fitting in. It must be a personal challenge for us to constantly build a feeling of belonging. Internal or external comfort only comes when we belong to ourselves and not to others. Married or single, our responsibility is to make ourselves become part of the mainstream of the Church. Comfort in some such instances may most effectively come as we labor to fit in and lose self.

5. *Prayer is power.*

Praying does more than rest the weary. It is a means of comforting the soul under all circumstances. What a comfort it has been to millions over the years to read what the Lord said in response to the plea of a discouraged Joseph Smith when he was in Liberty Jail in Missouri and cried out in anguish: "O God, where art thou? And where is the pavilion that covereth thy hiding place? How long shall thy hand be stayed, and thine eye, yea thy pure eye, behold from the eternal heavens the wrongs of thy people and of thy servants, and thine ear be penetrated with their cries?"

What joy, comfort, reassurance, and hope come from the Lord's response: "My son, peace be unto thy soul; thine adversity and thine afflictions shall be but a small moment;

and then, if thou endure it well, God shall exalt thee on high; thou shalt triumph over all thy foes." (D&C 121:1–2, 7–8.)

Prayer can well be a proper beginning and ending in our quest for comfort.

Ann Laemmlen shares this wholesome insight: "When I would pray and pray to know what to do next in my life, the answer always seemed to come, again and again, that my duties would be made plain. That was reassuring, but it didn't answer my questions. I wanted to know specifically what those duties were. Through all of this I have learned that God is not a distributor of answers. He is a creator of situations leading to the exaltation of his children. As I work with this process, I am becoming a better person, and I am learning to develop absolute trust in the Lord." (*A Singular Life,* pp. 46–47.)

I also love what Mary Ellen Edmunds has written on this subject: "One thing that has helped me very much through all the ups and downs of all the years of my life has been the knowledge that God lives and that I can communicate with him any time. Prayer has been such a significant source of help, comfort, peace, and direction. I like to pray specifically, to think, ponder, and listen. It means a lot to me when there's time to spend an hour or so and have a real dialogue rather than a monologue. . . .

"I am deeply grateful for the privilege of attending the temple. The blessings of being in that holy place increase my peace and fortify me for all that's outside in the world waiting for me. Temple attendance helps me gain perspective, understanding, and insight. I feel spiritually enlightened when I'm there. I love to see friends there; it is one

141

of the best places to run into someone you love. Temples have always seemed like places of refuge and sanctuary to me. I find answers to questions, a lightening of my burdens, and a wonderful sense of comfort while I'm there." (*A Singular Life,* pp. 151, 152.)

Temples are special houses where prayer, pondering, meditating, and associations bring comfort and peace. Seek comfort in sacred places. Take comfort to the temple with you.

6. *We can learn to endure well.*

Enduring is not tolerating. Enduring is moving forward with conviction and purpose under all circumstances. My good friend Carol Clark gives us a meaningful glimpse of enduring and its accompanying comforts:

"I often think of my own life as a series of options, each choice leading me down another path. . . . I still feel deep wells of longing for my husband and our children, but I more patiently accept my journey through life when I am spiritually in control, not in the midst of a spiritual tantrum because I still want-what-I-want-when-I-want-it. . . .

"Now a more seasoned traveler, I know that the real fun of life is in overcoming obstacles while still happily hoping everything will work out. . . . No one, nothing is going to ruin my life. I am the heroine of my odyssey, and I'll rise triumphant. My mettle has been sufficiently tested that I can say with surety, I will overcome anything. I freely admit that living with my dreams unfulfilled has proven to be a softening, humbling influence because it's been so hard. But the anchor is at hand, and because it is, I can progress, even though to date I've lost at love — the one thing I've wanted more in life than anything else save righteousness itself. . . .

"Last summer I complained to a non-Latter-day Saint friend that I was exhausted, having no fun, living like an automaton. Nonsympathetically, she countered, 'What do you think this is? A dress rehearsal? This is your life, Carol. Fix it.' I expected a pat and a kind word. Instead, I got a splash of reality square in the face. She was, of course, quite right. I wasn't giving my life value, so I didn't feel it had value. I went home, reread the parables of the sower and of the talents, and regrouped." (A *Singular Life*, pp. 35, 36.)

Carol Clark has life priorities that appeal to me—always ladylike, always sensitive to others, intelligent in her approaches and courageous in carrying them out. How comforting it is to me personally to associate with people like her who are stronger than their challenges.

Here are some additional thoughts that are priceless:

"Seeing myself progress and overcome challenges has brought me the most happiness in life. . . . That phrase, 'endure to the end,' has been used lightly so often that it may sound like a cliché. But I firmly believe that the principle of endurance that the prophets have taught from the beginning of time is not only a requirement for exaltation but also the secret to real happiness in this life." (Rebecca Coombs, in A *Singular Life*, pp. 23, 24.)

"Being of a basically stubborn nature, I determined years ago I would not allow anybody to drive me away from *my* church. Single, married, widowed, or divorced, I felt I had as much right and claim to it as any other person—and no one was going to take it away from me or drive me out. In the process of making that decision I learned to separate the 'church,' that is, individuals and institutional practices,

from the 'gospel,' that is, eternal principles and doctrine."
(Ida Smith, in *A Singular Life,* p. 101.)

7. *The Holy Ghost will comfort us in times of pain and trial.*

A wise stake president describes well the ministration power of the Holy Ghost: "Part of our earthly progression is to experience pain and suffering and disappointments. The Holy Ghost was meant to comfort us *through* sorrow, not necessarily to remove the experience of suffering. We need to learn this; otherwise, during suffering, we may start to disbelieve the Holy Ghost because we still hurt. . . . He doesn't take the pain away, but he gives [us] comfort." (Quoted by Jeanie McAllister in *A Singular Life,* p. 10.)

Marion Jane Cahoon's declaration rings with truth and power: "As a single person, I've never been particularly depressed that my garden hasn't yielded a bridal bouquet yet. Instead of focusing on the flowers that aren't there, I've chosen to truly savor the flowers that have bloomed. . . . Some blooms were cultivated opportunities; some were purely spontaneous. No matter how they came into my life, I have learned that my joy in the harvest increases when I focus on the beauty that is right at my feet instead of daydreaming about something else I'd like to see bloom in my life. . . .

"Instead of being worried over the Lord's timing, over the seasons and blooms and harvesting times in my garden, I have tried to simplify my approach by asking myself one question, one that Heavenly Father can give a confirmation to: 'What is the next right thing to do?' " (In *A Singular Life,* pp. 74, 83–84.)

"Belle S. Spafford said, 'A woman's reach is bounded

144

only by what her mind accepts and her heart allows.' I am continually discovering that my happiness or sadness depends upon the beliefs in my heart and mind because these ideas determine how I interpret my daily experiences. That is why I can be in the same situation as another and yet have a much different experience. Yes, it's my beliefs that will allow me to hang onto the feelings produced by the experiences I've just had." (Shelley Swain, in A *Singular Life*, p. 128.)

We are living in a day and time when comfort is necessary and is possible for all of us. Comfort is not easy to come by, but it is helpful to know we can attain it and how it is found. May it come and remain by our proper use of basic principles.

CHAPTER 17

To Those Who Are Returning

Some time ago a new friend, not then a member of the Church because of recent discipline, asked, "What can I do while I am waiting? Over the past period of time it has been made very evident what I cannot do. Tell me and others in my situation what we can do."

I recall vividly and with feeling this friend's additional request: "Please don't tell me to be patient, loving, sweet, and understanding. I need more than that. I need solid direction. I have an urgent need to get over my frustrated feelings and get on with life. Please help me."

As I try to respond to this sincere plea from a good person, perhaps I am directing my suggestions only to a few, but they are a precious few. I would endeavor to instill hope instead of despair in those who have temporarily lost certain powers and privileges. Some of these people in this category dare not hope anymore for fear of being disappointed. May they and their families be helped with thoughts that will bring action, comfort, and a new sense of self-worth. How can we as Church members best help these good people?

I suggest a quotation from the Book of Mormon as a foundation for our actions: "Nevertheless, ye shall not cast him out from among you, but ye shall minister unto him and shall pray for him unto the Father, in my name; and if it so be that he repenteth and is baptized in my name, then shall ye receive him, and shall minister unto him of my flesh and blood." (3 Nephi 18:30.)

Often in the scriptures we are reminded that we should minister to all of God's children and that we should do so with the pure love of God in our hearts. George Bernard Shaw once wrote, "The worst sin towards our fellow creatures is not to hate them, but to be indifferent to them." (*The Devil's Disciple*, act 2.) Indifference can be one of the most hurtful ways of behavior. Never should we allow ourselves to turn away, walk on the other side of the street, and pretend we didn't see, or prohibit involvement in accepted ways. We need to learn to love everyone, even those who are difficult.

A warm handshake and a friendly smile can be wonderfully healing medicine. Conversely, how unwise we are when we declare, "I'll never speak to him again." Never is a long time, and even those who have caused heartache or shame are not beyond ultimate repentance. Sometimes hurts to the heart are more damaging than physical blows. Yes, they may take longer to heal, but they will heal more quickly if we avoid bitterness and anger and practice forgiveness.

As we support the efforts of those who are trying to work through their challenges, we should be helpful; and we will be if we extend kindness, compassion, patience, and love.

Many of those who are waiting have been hurt by thoughtless words and deeds of those around them. Blessed is the person who avoids being offended. There are appropriate and acceptable assignments that can and should be given to those who are in this waiting period.

In the Book of Mormon we are given this warm invitation: "Yea, verily I say unto you, if ye will come unto me ye shall have eternal life. Behold, mine arm of mercy is extended towards you, and whosoever will come, him will I receive; and blessed are those who come unto me." (3 Nephi 9:14.)

This scripture indicates that in life there is no waiting period before we can come unto God. In our weakness we know where we can turn for strength. What good advice and wise direction for our lives can be gleaned through study of the scriptures! Self-esteem can be renewed and strength to do his will can be revived. People must always count more than programs.

As individuals come unto Christ, they learn of the reality of forgiveness: "Behold, he who has repented of his sins, the same is forgiven, and I, the Lord, remember them no more. By this ye may know if a man repenteth of his sins — behold, he will confess them and forsake them." (D&C 58:42–43.)

When people are convinced of the truth of the Lord's assurance that he will remember their sins no more, they are ready to start coming back to full fellowship. Some suggestions can be made using two effective words: *shun* and *participate. Shun* means to avoid deliberately and especially consistently, to abhor. To participate, one takes part or has a share in common with others.

We recommend that one should—

1. *Shun feelings of resentment, bitterness, and contention toward individuals rendering decisions.*

When discipline is administered, there is a tendency on the part of some to become resentful toward the individuals and institutions who have had to make the judgment. We should permit ourselves to take a self-inventory sampling before we "cast the first stone." Resentment and anger are not good for the soul. They are foul things. Bitterness must be replaced with humility. Truly, bitterness injures the one who carries it. It blinds, shrivels, and cankers.

Some of us are inclined to look to the weaknesses and shortcomings of others in order to expand our own comfort zone. To be effective, a worthy personal support system in cases like this must include family, friends, and acquaintances who are willing to help us cope with what we see and experience.

Moroni gave us all some words of advice: "Condemn me not because of mine imperfection, neither my father, because of his imperfection, neither them who have written before him; but rather give thanks unto God that he hath made manifest unto you our imperfections, that ye may learn to be more wise than we have been." (Mormon 9:31.)

Repentant individuals will choose their own course and proceed with confidence. They have no need to protect a wounded self. They will not allow themselves the danger of self-inflicted sympathy. It is generally good medicine to sympathize with others, but not with oneself.

2. *Shun discouragement.*

One of Satan's most powerful tools is discouragement. Whisperings of "you can't do it," "you're no good," "it's too late," "what's the use?" or "things are hopeless" are tools of destruction. Satan would like us to believe that because we've made one mistake, it's all over. He wants us

149

to quit trying. It is important that discouragement be cast out of the lives of those who are waiting. This may take work and energy, but it can be accomplished.

3. *Shun escape routes.*

There are those who would welcome us into rebellious or apostate groups. We can never build with purpose if we join the ranks of those who criticize and aim to tear down.

It is easier to demean and place blame on others for our situation than it is to repent and grow. Some who set out to damage and destroy others end up losing themselves in the process. Drugs, alcoholic beverages, pornographic materials, and subculture associations are also escape routes. Attitudes of "it won't matter now" or "there's nothing for you to do" are totally inappropriate. "Pure religion and undefiled before God and the Father is this, To visit the fatherless and widows in their affliction, and to keep himself unspotted from the world." (James 1:27.) Maintaining and building require discipline and patience. We must shun those who would build themselves by destroying others.

4. *Shun the desire to become anonymous.*

When difficulties arise, some want to fade into the crowd and become lost and unknown. Any thinking person will realize that a wonderful support system is available to those who are listed on the records of the Church. There are those who will listen, help, and teach. There will be opportunities to study scriptures, ponder, and pray. Caring people and a caring God want to know where we are.

All people need to be known, recognized, and loved. Hearts and souls reach out for nurturing and meaningful association. Even those who claim they just want to be left alone are in reality seeking their own identity.

Some privileges and powers are lost when we lose our membership in the Church, but let us not lose ourselves in the process of finding ourselves again. In God's eyes, nobody is a nobody. We should never lose sight of what we may become and who we are.

5. *Participate with your family.*

Family members are priceless possessions. They offer love and strength. But even more, family members need each other. We can choose to be aware of the needs of each family member and do our part to help fill those needs. Some need a person to listen; some may need a compliment or positive reinforcement. There is strength and satisfaction in becoming involved in family projects. We can encourage family love by being approachable even when we feel we have reason to turn away. The first step back in seeking family acceptance is to change oneself for the better. It is true today, true yesterday, and will be true tomorrow that effective leadership can only be administered through love.

6. *Participate in Church functions and meetings.*

Those who are waiting should accept opportunities to take appropriate assignments when given the opportunity. I will always be grateful to a good man who helped our boys while it was not possible for him to take part in all the Church programs. He was well loved, and he loved the boys to whom he gave time and guidance.

We all need to practice dependability and commitment and adapt to existing conditions. There are places to serve where we are needed. When someone declares, "There's nothing for me to do," it just isn't true. We sometimes make that statement because we have learned to live with present situations and resist new opportunities. Leaders must always be sensitive enough to look beyond restrictions and policies to the ultimate long-range needs of God's children.

7. *Participate in worthy community projects, including compassionate and other volunteer services.*

Often our own problems seem to diminish when we become aware of the challenges faced by others. When my wife was volunteering as a pink lady at one of our local hospitals, she noticed that some of the doctors in the area would encourage their patients who were depressed, sad, or emotionally ill to join the volunteer organization. That prescription often worked better than medicine in building self-image and restoring health to those who found joy in helping others.

As budget cuts limit so many of our cultural and civic programs, there is a place for anyone who desires to work with Scouts, help with reputable charitable drives to collect money, and help in schools, art galleries, welfare agencies, and many other places. There are no restrictions on participating in good works. There are no reasons to wait while God's children are in need of our love and service. Love should be a vehicle allowed to travel without limitations.

8. *Participate in "reporting in."*

Part of everyone's responsibility in coming back is to find someone with whom they can share their concerns, questions, and progress. John Powell, in his book *The Secret of Staying in Love,* tells us that "the genius of communication is the ability to be both totally honest and totally kind at the same time." (Valencia, California: Tabor Publishing, 1974, p. 131.)

We should look for this kind of person in our lives. Problems often seem to diminish when they are vocalized.

Another person's point of view may help us gain a different perspective of a situation. It is comforting to have a listener who will share our feelings and respect our needs. Communication should be kind, gentle, open, and constructive.

One of the greatest blessings available to all is personal prayer. By this means everyone can "report in" to an understanding Father who loves all his children. God knows the feelings in every human heart. He can soften sorrow and lead when there seems to be no light. Prayer can give guidance and confidence. It reminds us that no one need be alone in this world. If all else fails, remember: God and one other person can be a family.

My plea and invitation to all, especially to those who have temporarily lost certain privileges, is to come back. One of the main goals of the Church is to secure the development and happiness of the individual. President David O. McKay once wrote: "In thus emphasizing individual effort, I am not unmindful of the necessity of cooperation. A single, struggling individual may be stalled with his heavy load even as he begins to climb the hill before him. To reach the top unaided is an impossibility. With a little help from fellow travelers he makes the grade and goes on his way in gratitude and rejoicing." (*Pathways to Happiness*, Salt Lake City: Bookcraft, 1957, p. 181.)

To those who are returning, I would say: We want to be your fellow travelers while you are en route back. Anxiously engage in actions and attitudes that will bring full fellowship and the accompanying joys and rights to which you will be entitled. We will be at your side to help as you travel upward in a support system with God at the helm.

CHAPTER 18

Focus on the Future

John Wooden retired after forty years of coaching college basketball. During the twenty-seven years he coached at the University of California at Los Angeles, his teams never had a losing season. They won ten national championships. He often said, "The mark of a true champion is to always perform near your own level of competency. We were able to do that by never being satisfied with the past and always planning for what was to come. This constant focus on the future is one reason we continued staying near the top once we got there." Then he added, "Success isn't outscoring someone, it's the peace of mind that comes from self-satisfaction in knowing you did your best."

For each of us, various chapters in our lives close as we graduate from school, are married, or move on to new circumstances in other ways. But always, the game of life stretches out before us. We must not look back, but focus on the future.

The game of life isn't easy. Dr. Scott Peck, in *The Road Less Traveled,* has written: "Life is difficult. This is a great truth, one of the greatest truths. Once we truly know that life is difficult — once we truly understand and accept it —

154

then life is no longer difficult. Because once it is accepted, the fact that life is difficult no longer matters. . . . Life is a series of problems. Do we want to moan about them or solve them?" (New York: Simon and Schuster, 1978, p. 15.)

There is fun and satisfaction in conquering challenges that are difficult. A well-worn proverb tells us, "Failing to prepare is preparing to fail." We each need to learn where our own level of competency is, then strive to perform at our best. However, our level of competency can increase all through our life.

It has been accurately and wisely observed that man has two creators: God and himself. God obviously did a good job in creating each of us. Now what are we going to do with ourselves? What traits and skills am I going to develop as I create a better *me*?

In this quest for self-improvement, may I offer a few suggestions.

First, it is important that we extend our learning. As long as there is life, education in one form or another never ceases. Oliver Hertford said: "The great American myth is that when someone is handed the skin of a dead sheep at graduation time, it will keep his mind alive forever." "Use it or lose it" applies to our brains as well as to our muscles.

In the Doctrine and Covenants we are advised: "If a person gains more knowledge and intelligence in this life through his diligence and obedience than another, he will have so much the advantage in the world to come." (D&C 130:19.) The Lord encourages us to pursue education for temporal advantage and eternal progression. Education is not a posture, stance, or recognition. It is, in fact, a continuing process. When learning is applied properly, it can become power. Wisdom and integrity must become an integral part of a truly educated person. Education is not an arrival achievement. It is a journey.

If we will observe and even copy work habits and life patterns of wise, good, successful people, we can garner much sound judgment. It will help us make correct application of knowledge. Longfellow confirms this thought in his poem "A Psalm of Life":

> Lives of great men all remind us
> We can make our lives sublime
> And, departing, leave behind us
> Footprints in the sands of time.

Another source for added education is the scriptures. There is pertinent counsel in the words of Nephi: "O the vainness, and the frailties, and the foolishness of men! When they are learned they think they are wise, and they hearken not unto the counsel of God, for they set it aside, supposing they know of themselves, wherefore, their wisdom is foolishness and it profiteth them not. And they shall perish. But to be learned is good if they hearken unto the counsels of God." (2 Nephi 9:28–29.) As life unfolds, none of us should get so busy that we forget to study the scriptures and the words of our prophets. As specific needs come into our lives, wisdom that was formerly unseen is there to give us added knowledge.

Mortimer Adler, who was acclaimed worldwide as a great educator, indicated in an interview that his education had begun just a few years before that interview. The interviewer, surprised, said, "But you are famous for the many years you were associated with the University of Chicago."

156

Mr. Adler responded, "Those years I was obtaining my schooling. It was only after I had finished my formal schooling that my education began."

Living in the world can broaden horizons, expand understanding, and increase tolerance if we learn from our experiences and look for good in all people.

A second bit of advice, as we focus on the future, is to stay in control of appetites, passions, and emotions. Somehow, when we see others mess up their lives with unwise choices and foolish actions, we think "That will never happen to me." I quote some famous words: "There are a thousand steps from hell to heaven, but only one step from heaven to hell!"

Day after day these words are verified by news reports of scams, cheating, lying, murders, and drug addiction. Each year thousands are killed or maimed by drunken drivers, but only when an acquaintance is involved in such a tragedy does the impact become real. Only when one is involved does that one step from heaven to hell become horribly apparent. Drugs drag bright, healthy people into an awful hell. Addicts, at the mercy of their uncontrollable cravings, rob, murder, and commit all sorts of heinous crimes. Family, friends, and professions take a back seat to intense desires for "fixes." Lives are ruined. That first wrong step indeed leads to hell.

But, you say, that won't happen to me — or will it?

Reason can also be paralyzed by anger. Loss of temper and uncontrolled rage can wipe away self-control. A violent act may cause a person to lose control of his life. To reach our highest level of competency, each of us must learn to govern our temper and passions. If we don't, they control us. Emotional control can save a situation that might deteriorate into disaster. The power of persuasion works better than authoritarian actions, which diminish another's self-esteem. In the Doctrine and Covenants, the Lord warns us that if we come in contact with a spirit that is not of God, we are to proclaim against that spirit: "Not with railing accusations, that ye be not overcome, neither with boasting nor rejoicing, lest you be seized therewith." (D&C 50:32–33.)

Another potent admonition we would do well to remember is this one: "A soft answer turneth away wrath; but grievous words stir up anger." (Proverbs 15:1.)

Sooner or later those who are not trustworthy hinder forward progress. Those who lie, cheat, or misrepresent slowly but surely weave a web that will so encase them that eventually they lose control, are at the mercy of the law or those they injure, and can no longer win in the game of life. Again, first steps on the wrong path only lead downward.

Telling the truth makes a person truthful. Telling a lie makes a person a liar. Trust is not a magic quality that can be acquired by the wave of a wand. It can't be inherited from our parents. It has to be earned. But when we become known as being trustworthy, many doors will open and many advantages will be ours.

The development of character through self-mastery is part of the game plan of life's winners. What is wrong with treating ourselves as first-class persons? We can do this if we have self-respect, self-pride, and self-discipline, and if we manage ourselves, govern our appetites, and control our passions so that we can give our best effort and achieve our highest level of competency. Lasting joy can come to those who are willing to pay the price of self-denial to achieve a noble character and reach lofty goals. Let us strive for the peace of mind that comes from being in charge of ourselves.

Although there are many other things we might consider as we focus on the future, the last factor I shall mention is to focus on the future with a positive mental attitude, to be enthusiastic and excited about life. Ralph Waldo Emerson wrote, "Nothing great was ever achieved without enthusiasm!" Enthusiasm and a positive mental attitude are mandatory for great accomplishments in life.

Researchers at the Peak Performance Center in California have found that those who are most successful enjoy many facets of life. They love life, they love beauty, and they have many friends. They are excited about the possibilities that are available.

Good advice is given to us in Romans 14:22: "Hast thou faith? have it to thyself before God. Happy is he that condemneth not himself in the thing which he alloweth." We should strive for that wholesome balance available from education, God, good health habits, and friends.

People who internalize their personal worth will attempt more and achieve more than those who do not. Most of us see what we are looking for. Life is full of beauty and opportunities; there are also dark corners and sordid events. Let us be aware of the unsavory possibilities and face life realistically, but let us also be excited about opportunities and relish the beautiful. If we plant beautiful, positive, correct thoughts and ideas in our minds, that is what we will harvest. The Lord has promised, "According to your desires, yea, even according to your faith shall it be done to you." (D&C 11:17.)

It is important to set high but not impossible goals. This means we have to know ourselves and our talents and abilities. We shouldn't be too modest, but we should realistically decide on our options and then plan our course of action. Everyone must have a road map and a means of transportation to complete a successful journey.

Senator John Stennis, who served forty-one years in the United States Senate, said, "I'll plow a straight furrow to the end of my row." Yet he had to overcome many road blocks. He lost a leg to cancer and had heart surgery and other health problems. He declared, "I learn to have courage to reach goals when I am taught from others who have overcome and achieved."

May I also remind you of the importance of self-esteem. Too many failures are brought about by the disconcerting feeling that others are better and more worthy than we are. If we become locked in a prison of low esteem and self-pity, only we hold the key to unlock that heavy door. We should each think well of ourselves and proclaim this fact to the world and our associates, not in loud words but in great deeds. Each of us must accept the fact that every individual is a child of a loving Heavenly Father. Each has a mission. Each is needed. Each can make the world better.

Christ has told us that we are the light of the world. He loves us as we are. He knows what we can become. We are usually blessed with good examples and helping hands all around us, yet God expects all of his children to make their own decisions, knowing that each person, in the end, must be accountable and responsible for his or her own actions.

Let us stride into the future with determination and

confidence. Sometimes people have doubts and worry about the uncertainty of the future. This is not new. The unknown has always brought doubts and wonder. But dreams have always been realized through individual effort and commitment. To make dreams come true, there is a process. It is achieved step by step, day by day, and month by month. Self-reliance and dedication, with a willingness to work long and hard and with patience, must be our way of life. Being true and faithful to righteous principles will always bring happiness.

Many people today have a tendency to seek instant pleasure, instant relief, instant change, instant success, instant wealth, omitting the day-by-day effort. Then they become discouraged if goals are not reached immediately. Disraeli once asked, "Have you ever watched a stonecutter at work? He will hammer away at a rock for one hundred times without a crack showing in it. Then on the one hundred and first blow the rock will split in two. It is not that blow alone, the one hundred and first blow that accomplished the results, but the hundred others that went before it as well."

Each of us is sometimes discouraged at how long it takes to learn something. We resent the practice necessary to become proficient. But effort is not lost. Mastery is a little closer with each effort expended.

Let us focus on the future, and learn in every available way through study, work, reasoning, and prayer. Great things are wrought by prayer and faith, after all we can do. As Tennyson wrote, "More things are wrought by prayer than this world dreams of." May we plan for the future and plan to succeed. Even with good intentions and wise plans,

161

challenges and trials are bound to come into every life. When they do, let us not ask, Why did this happen to me? Rather, let us replace that question of despair with: What does this situation require of me? How can I solve this problem?

May I conclude with one more stanza from "A Psalm of Life":

> Not enjoyment, and not sorrow
> Is our destined end or way;
> But to act that each tomorrow
> Finds us farther than today.

May God bless each of us as we go forward.

Sources

Chapter 1, "The Measure of Our Hearts": general conference address, October 1988.

Chapter 2, "I Would Be Worthy": general conference address, April 1989.

Chapter 3, "For There Are Many Gifts": general conference address, October 1987.

Chapter 4, "That's Just the Way I Am": address to Lambda Delta Sigma and Sigma Gamma Chi, Salt Lake Tabernacle, September 10, 1989.

Chapter 5, "A Pattern in All Things": general conference address, October 1990.

Chapter 6, "Lessons from the Master": Brigham Young University devotional address, June 1988.

Chapter 7, "I Will Not Boast of Myself": general conference address, April 1990.

Chapter 8, "How Much Attention Is Fair?": film-lecture series, Church Office Building, October 21, 1983.

Chapter 9, "He Loveth That Which Is Right": seventeen-stake fireside address, Brigham Young University, March 5, 1989.

Chapter 10, "Learning to School Our Feelings": address at Missionary Training Center, Provo, Utah, June 19, 1990.

Chapter 11, "A Voice of Perfect Mildness": general priesthood meeting address, September 1989.

Chapter 12, "Stalwart and Brave We Stand": general priesthood meeting address, September 1989.

Sources

Chapter 13, "Receiving Answers to Our Prayers": address at Missionary Training Center, Provo, Utah, November 24, 1987.

Chapter 14, "Get In and Get Involved": commencement address, Ricks College, April 21, 1983.

Chapter 15, "A Voice of Gladness": general conference address, April 1991.

Chapter 16, "For Those Who Stand in Need": address at BYU Women's Conference, April 8, 1988.

Chapter 17, "To Those Who Are Returning": general conference address, April 1988.

Chapter 18, "Focus on the Future": commencement address, Brigham Young University, April 28, 1989.

Index

165